From Pulwama to Payback

BALAKOT

THE INSIDE STORY

FRANCESCA MARINO

Vitasta

Published by
Renu Kaul Verma
Vitasta Publishing Pvt Ltd
4348/4C, Ansari Road, Daryaganj
New Delhi - 110 002
info@vitastapublishing.com

ISBN: 978-81-988295-9-7
©Francesca Marino
First Edition 2025
MRP 495

All Rights Reserved.
No part of this publication may be reproduced, stored in a retrieval system, or transmitted in any form, or by any means–electronic, mechanical, photocopying, recording or otherwise–without the prior permission of the publisher. Opinions expressed in this book are the authors' own. The publisher is in no way responsible for these.

Edited by Sandhya Sridhar
Layout by Shubhpreet Kaur
Cover Design by Smriti Maheshwari
Printed by Vikas Computer and Printers, New Delhi

To

Milind Kelkar, who was called too soon
and could not wait for the book to be out.
And to Renu, Gauri and Akshay Kelkar,
the family of my heart.

The only line a journalist is required to follow is the railway line

—Albert Londres

CONTENTS

Introduction	xi
We Attacked!	1
Drawing Maps	19
Of Walls and Enemies	34
India's Brain	48
A Terror Enterprise	69
Of Terror and Training	87
Srinagar is Still Beautiful	110
Links with Taliban	138
Jihadi Social	151
"No War, No Peace"	171
Postscript: When History Writes Back	185

INTRODUCTION

I was in second grade when in an essay titled 'What I will do when I grow up', I wrote that I would become a journalist and a writer. This decision was reaffirmed when a couple of years later, a book by Oriana Fallaci about the Vietnam War came into my hands. The book was titled *Nothing and So Be It*, and on the cover was a black-and-white photo of Oriana in pigtails and a military helmet. 'I want to be that,' I remember thinking, and I have not changed my mind since.

I devoured old movies and books on journalism and journalists, read everything that came my way, whether it was age-appropriate or not. Books, magazines and newspapers have been the best and most cherished companions of my childhood and teenage, when I was living in a small town in the South of Italy, dreaming only to leave and explore the world. Oddly enough, I was never interested in the "glamour" part of journalism, and I never thought for a moment about doing anything other than taking a plane or a train, going to a place and reporting—immersing myself in places where life and people were different from what I knew.

"The Elsewhere"—places unexplained or insufficiently explained. Places I longed to understand. Places where things were happening but were rarely spoken about, or when they were, it was poorly and superficially—at least in Italy. Albert Londres' phrase that opens this book, "The only line that a journalist is required to follow is the railway line" has always been my mantra. So too, did Londres' reportage inspire me and continues to inspire me even today. It is so even now, when this line of work has become internationally something completely different, and for me, frankly, alien. When before reporting or writing you have to adhere to the social and political agenda of the editorial board, and to the now ubiquitous "political correctness". When your articles are scrutinised—especially in most Anglo-Saxon newspapers—not just for factual accuracy, but for the appropriateness of language and expressed opinions. When prestigious prizes are awarded to news inventors because the scrutiny is not necessarily done on the truth of a story, but for how carefully the narratives are conveyed. All this means that there is a problem. In the modern world, a masterpiece like Truman Capote's *In Cold Blood* would never have been published or appreciated, just as the journalists who broke the Watergate scandal would not have passed the scrutiny of virtuous verifiers demanding impeccably cross-referenced sources.

Years ago, a colleague trying to insult me, told me that I had an "ethical conception" of journalism that was outdated and not in keeping with today's world. All these and more, stories and reflections that would have little to do with this book, however, came back to me when I published my articles on Balakot. The reactions triggered by the publication of my stories, taught me a lot. About the way this work is done nowadays. About "professional racism" practised against Italian or European journalists in general (the ones who are not native English speakers): a confirmation, should I need another one, of a deeply entrenched bias.

In March 2001, my late husband Sergio Trippodo, Beniamino Natale, Paolo Grassini and the Pakistani Nafees Thakar embarked, in quite a daring trip, all the way to Bamiyan. They were the last ones to shoot the Buddhas while they were still standing. But when they tried to sell the footage to various international news outlets, the answer invariably was, 'How is it possible you did it, while we could not?' And that was the end of the story. Nobody wanted the footage, which the foursome made later into a documentary only for the Italian audience. The same thing happened when I tried to sell to an American publication, my interview with Mohammed Hafiz Saeed, the LeT Amir. The same thing happened with Balakot as well.

Balakot taught me a lot about professional ethics and also about friendship, or so-called ones. The experience has made me perhaps much more cynical, and certainly stronger. This book is the result of years of research, just as the articles about Balakot were the result of years of practising the profession and of the relationships woven over those years. This book is also the outcome of my connections with those persons, or rather the people who told me (and continue to tell me) facts and events from places where it is usually not possible or difficult for a Westerner (and sometimes also for a citizen of the country) to have access. I established such contacts during the years I spent in the countries I reported from, by talking to the official powers, and also by mixing with ordinary people. I "got my hands dirty" in person, always. Plus, whenever and wherever I could, I stood at international conferences and institutional spaces, speaking for the oppressed people of the land I was covering. I denounced human rights abuses, political motivated violence, enforced disappearances and extrajudicial killings of Baloch, Pashtun and Sindhi.

Finally, as I always do, I try to write for ordinary people, for those who without being specialists, are interested in the topic at hand. For those who seek facts—facts speak for themselves without the need for opinions on the subject. As always, I have tried as much as I could to entrust the telling of events to the voices of the protagonists, rather than confining the narrative to my own. I hope I have managed to tell a piece of recent history, news of the Indian subcontinent, without ideological or political bias, by sticking only to the famous railway line. And above all, I hope I have managed to tell the story without boring the readers: for this, really, is an unethical and an unforgivable sin.

WE ATTACKED!

'We attacked!'

My old friend Praveen Swami sounded quite excited as I picked up his call, still half asleep.

It was barely five o'clock in the morning in Rome. It was still dark outside on the very cold morning of 26 February 2019. I was still in bed.

'Wake up!' insisted Praveen. 'Wake up and start calling your contacts. See if somebody has seen something.'

'We, who? Seen what?' I could barely mumble. 'And where?'

'Balakot, Pakistan! Start calling!'

I pressed the start button of the coffee maker that stood on the night table beside me, trying to push sleep away. The last time I had been woken up in the middle of the night was when I had received a call from Pakistan many years before, when the Americans landed in Abbottabad.

I started checking my phone numbers, and began making calls.

With a certain sadistic pleasure, I must say, I also started waking up my contacts all over Europe.

'Wake up! India has attacked a terrorist camp in Pakistan!'

Before my coffee was ready, and before the first light of the day had entered my room, I was already at work. It was clear from the beginning that narratives had almost immediately taken the place of mere facts.

The facts were apparently quite simple. A number of Indian aircraft had entered Khyber Pakhtunkhwa (KPK) airspace, dropped a load of bombs on Balakot, a well-known Jaish-e-Mohammed (JeM) terrorist camp in Pakistan, and flown back without any acknowledgment from the Pakistani Army.

From the official statement of Indian Foreign Secretary VK Gokhale:

> Credible intelligence was received that JeM was attempting another suicide terror attack in various parts of the country, and the fidayeen jihadis were being trained for this purpose. In the face of imminent danger, a preemptive strike became absolutely necessary. In an intelligence-led operation in the early hours of today, India struck the biggest training camp of JeM in Balakot. In this operation, a very large number of JeM terrorists, trainers, senior commanders and groups of jihadis who were being trained for fidayeen action were eliminated. This facility at Balakot was headed by Maulana Yousuf Azhar (alias Ustad Ghouri), the brother-in-law of Masood Azhar, Chief of JeM.

My first reaction, I must say, was to laugh. Laugh a lot.

Many years before in London, when I was discussing the Abbottabad story with former Pakistani President Pervez Musharraf, I had told him, 'If you want me to believe that American helicopters entered Pakistani airspace (on 2 May 2011) without being detected, landed in a military citadel, killed Osama bin Laden, blasted one of their helicopters, and then returned while your Army and Intelligence people were sleeping, God help you if India one day decides to do the same.'

One of the explanations Musharraf had given to me in his fairly angry reply, was that the bulk of their military forces were focussed on the Indian border, which they saw as their primary threat—and not on the Afghan border. But in reality, that wasn't true. Because the state of their defence systems, particularly their radar capabilities during the Balakot raids, were clearly in the same conditions as during the Abbottabad raid (the joke back then was: AAA for sale! Anti Aircraft Artillery radar—does not detect military helicopters, but can catch Star TV!).

However, something had changed. The era of social media had bloomed. The legendary Major General Asif "Burnol" Ghafoor was Pakistan's Director-General, Inter-Services Public Relations (ISPR), and was also running a flourishing troll factory from Rawalpindi.

So this time, unlike during the Abbottabad incident, there was a befitting and prompt (although confused) reply from the Pakistani forces. At least on social media.

First, Pakistan announced the intrusion of Indian aircraft into its airspace, but asserted that the Indian fleet was intercepted, causing them to retreat—to release their bombs which hit an open area, and to dump their fuel.

Then Ghafoor added that three IAF teams were spotted approaching the Pakistani border from various sectors in the early hours of 26 February. He also stated that two of these teams did not cross the border following a challenge from Pakistani combat air patrol, but that the third one crossed the Line of Control from Kiran Valley near Muzaffarabad, before being intercepted by Pakistani Air Force (PAF) jets within three minutes of the incursion.

Pervez Khattak, the then Pakistani Defence Minister, stated that the Pakistani Air Force did not retaliate at that time because "they could not gauge the extent of the damage".

However, according to former Air Chief Marshal Birender Singh Dhanoa who was in command of the Balakot operation, 'There was no Pakistani aircraft within 150 km of our strike package,' and the Pakistani Army, the "greatest army in the world" (even though it had actually never won a war) had once again been taken by complete surprise.

What followed was one of the biggest attempts to cover up and distort facts that we have seen in many years. It was difficult after the Abbottabad operation, to admit to the official version of the story—that the Americans had landed in Pakistan and killed Osama bin Laden (whose presence in the country Islamabad had always denied), while the Chief of Army and the ISI Chief were sound asleep in their homes. A Parliament Commission created *ad hoc* years later, settled the matter with a report that could be considered hilarious. But at the end of the day, as Musharraf and others have said, the whole thing was an unfortunate but tolerable breach—carried out, after all, by a "friendly" nation, a key ally in the so-called "war on terror".

But it's one thing to mislead your own public in deference to an ally like the United States. It's quite another to come to terms with the fact that India—"the Enemy Number One"—could execute a similarly bold operation, and do so with apparent impunity. The official response was swift and familiar—outright denial.

So let's summarise: Islamabad claimed that the Indian planes were repelled by those from Pakistan, who promptly responded. According to them, there had been no bombing, and the Indian operation had completely failed.

After the initial denials, however, Islamabad admitted that

the Indian MiGs, twelve in number, had apparently not only crossed the Line of Control (LoC) for the first time since 1971, but had also gone 130 miles into Pakistan to reach Balakot, KPK, not far from Abbottabad.

India declared that this was not an attack on Pakistan, but was aimed at the JeM and the jihadi training camps. The same camps that according to Islamabad, did not exist. Perhaps. Or rather, they existed depending on the convenience and the day.

We must remember that in the aftermath of the Pulwama attack that killed forty Indian soldiers, Pakistan had asked India for "credible evidences" of the involvement of Jaish-e-Mohammed, forgetting quite conveniently that JeM itself had admitted in two separate videos that they were responsible for the attack.

Coming back to Balakot, a few days later, while the Financial Action Task Force (FATF) once again debated whether Pakistan should be put on the blacklist of countries sponsoring terrorism, Islamabad declared to have banned the Jamaat-ud-Dawa and to have taken "administrative control" of the headquarters of JeM in Bahawalpur. The very same headquarters that did not exist until the day before.

Defying every sense of the absurd, two days later, the same Minister of Information who had issued the above statement took everything back, claiming that Balakot "is a madrasa. Indian propaganda says it is the headquarters of JeM". But of course, the sense of the absurd is not in the DNA of either the Government of Pakistan or the Islamabad Army. Both not only continued to beat the bass drum of the "best army in the world" despite never having won a war, but also continued to issue statements, then withdraw them without batting an eyelid. Lashkar-e-Toiba (LeT) and affiliates (including JuD), have in fact been banned innumerable times, and so has the JeM.

In the aftermath of the Mumbai attacks on 26 November 2008, for which Pakistan was given evidence of the involvement of the LeT both from India and the US, Islamabad had done the same thing with Muridke, the headquarters of LeT/JuD. The result? Muridke, since then, has been financed with public funds and continues to be the headquarters of Mohammed Hafiz Saeed.

On the other hand, for a very long time Pakistan had claimed to have no idea of where Osama bin Laden was. It also claimed to have no control over the Taliban co-founder Abdul Ghani Baradar, also known as Mullah Baradar and the Afghan Taliban.

Thus, the saraband of news, statements and declaration went on for days.

Hamid Mir, a famous Pakistani journalist, was rushed to the site of the bombing to show "crows and trees" allegedly hit by the Indian airplanes, as well as the four big craters in the middle of nowhere that were "hit" by the bombs. Mir then interviewed terrified villagers who swore they heard nothing, and went on to say that nobody was hurt or hit. Mir sold this version to all the international media. However, international media were stopped from getting close to the actual location of the bombing. They could send only their local stringers to the location.

Reuters stated in an article published 6 March 2019, that:

> On the wooded slopes above Jaba village near Balakot, residents pointed to four bomb craters and some splintered pine trees. But there were little other visible effects of the explosions that blasted them awake around 3 am. 'It shook everything,' said Abdur Rasheed, a van driver who lives in the area. He said there weren't any human casualties. 'No one died. Only some pine trees died, they were cut down. A crow also died.'.... Western diplomats in Islamabad also said they did not believe the Indian air force hit a militant camp. 'There was no militant

training camp there. It hasn't been there for a few years–they moved it. It's common knowledge amongst our intelligence,' said one of them.

The same Reuters would call me twice at one point, asking me how I could have found an eyewitness while their correspondent could not.

Meanwhile in India, TV channels and social media were busy discussing the operation. A great many of them led by the Congress-sponsored Karan Thapar, were trying hard to promote the Pakistani version of the story just to damage the BJP government in the time of elections. The rest of the media were trying to assess the success of the operation with various degrees of sensationalistic reports and informal intelligence inputs.

The Print described the operation thus:

At about 0115 hours on February 26, 2019, 20 fully armed Mirage 2000 fighter aircraft took off, one by one in quick succession, from the runway and taxiway of the Air Force Station at Gwalior. They flew towards Bareilly and tanked up mid-air, then headed towards Jammu and Kashmir. At about 0345 hours, the fighters, which were flying in the cover of mountains to escape a Pakistani SAAB Airborne Warning and Control aircraft, crossed the LoC at 30,000 feet. While 16 aircraft crossed into PoK—including four for escort duties—four others stayed behind as back-up. Five Israeli-made Spice 2000 bombs were released about 15 km into PoK, which struck the Jaish-e-Mohammed camp in Balakot, and the fighters made their way back to an airfield in the Western Sector. However, four Mirages—armed with Mica RF and IR air-to-air missiles—stayed back until the other 12 aircraft made their way back into Indian airspace, lest Pakistan fighters engaged.

The entire ops, from the aircraft entering PoK and landing back in India, lasted about 21 minutes. 'The choice of target and execution came with a lot of planning and intelligence inputs. It was important to send a message to Pakistan that India will not tolerate any more attacks like Pulwama.'

The media jamboree went on for days, becoming nastier as it progressed. It was made worse by the fact that the Indian government did not release any official proof of the operation.

'No military will part with classified information to win a propaganda war,' was the reply of former Indian Air Chief Marshal BS Dhanoa to one of my questions. He added:

> There is something known as information in the classified domain. Suppose I have some capability but I don't want to tell you my best capability… since our animosity with Pakistan is not over, I will not show you my capability. I will show you what is commercially available. Is quite simple: you never part with your capability until you stop using it. During the Kargil War we kept classified what we were doing, but when we got the Sukhoi 30 in numbers, we got the MiG-21 in numbers then we said, okay this is how we did it in Kargil, because we no longer used that system. As long as we are using that system, that particular method of attack and things like that cannot be declassified just to win a propaganda battle. What the international press was looking from us was a briefing in which we would declassify it and then release the pictures.

Therefore, there were no pictures and no official assessments other than the few lines given as a press brief.

While Asif "Burnol" Ghafoor and his team were showing dead birds, and reports of villagers mocking the operation, Indian news outlets like *The Wire* were headlining articles saying that Balakot was "a very precise miss". The number of victims, again according to the Indian media, was around 350, almost all residents of the Balakot terror facility. According to Pakistan, of course, there was nothing called a Balakot terrorist camp. It was just a madrasa for local children that stayed intact and untouched. Aerial pictures of the location were revealed both by official and unofficial sources, showing the buildings of the camps totally intact. 'The wrong buildings intact,' commented Dhanoa, who went on to state:

> The type of weapon makes a lot of difference, but the real question [was] since when were you prepared. We were prepared for a very long time. The weapon that was chosen is the one which has got maximum shrapnel and lower blasts. You see, when you go against the army, you want to flatten everything. So you go with weapons which have got higher explosive content, and here, if you go for this kind of target, we have more shrapnel. Basically you want to explode a cavity. Suppose this is a building, ideally the bomb should break through the roof and explode. It explodes here in the cavity, so that everybody in it will go.

But if it explodes on the roof, then the roof will fall in. But suppose I am under the table, nothing will happen to me. Or, I am lucky. I am in a corner, nothing will happen to me. So those kind of weapons are not used for this. We used a special weapon where you adjust the fuse. Physics—you know how thick is the concrete, what is the strength of the concrete so you keep the delay so much so it breaks, and this kind broke, but did not bury deep. It hit the floor and it exploded. So that could be one of the reasons the entry holes are clearly visible in commercial satellite imagery.

However, let's get into this and into Dhanoa's words a little later. As I said earlier, the saraband of news and counter-news, comments and opinions, went on for days. Both parties at times, for different reasons, were defying not only logic, but also common sense. They were obsessively trying to prove, in one way or the other, what had really happened that would fit their narrative, reaching paroxysms of hysteria.

Meanwhile, in Italy, I was busy studying and talking to people, trying to read between the propaganda from both sides, as to what had really happened, and of course, trying to fulfil Praveen's demands. And while the polemics were infuriating on any available platform, a few days later, I got a totally unexpected phone call, 'How are you, madam?'

The voice was a known one, I knew that voice for sure. But I could not place it immediately. It was a voice from the past.

Asif, and this of course was not his real name, was somebody I had known for ages. I had met his wife in the market at a bangle shop. His wife was with his mother, his sister, and his children. We started chatting. I played with the little girls, and then I was taken home for chai. For many years we shared food, laughs, and stories. Asif saved my life once. I will not tell you the whole story, for it might give away his identity. You can never be too careful.

I saved his little daughter's leg when she was hit and burned by a motorbike, a motorbike that rode away without stopping. I also acted as the "doctor" for all the ladies of the family for very, very long. They were happy times, thinking back. They were also times when I was more than welcome in Pakistan. It was not just the ordinary people, but also the top political class, a very good part of the Army and the ISI, who made me feel more than welcome.

I was very close to Asif and his family, until my travels to

Pakistan came to an abrupt stop. I stopped contacting people who could end up in trouble for being associated with me. In 2011, some smart brain in the ISI decided that I needed to be "taught a lesson". This was because I had refused twice, in Geneva and in Brussels, to peddle the lies on Kashmir served to European institutions, by Abdul Majid Tramboo and his Kashmir Centre. Above all, I was endorsing the Baloch protests and had started to become very vocal against the genocide in the region.

I was detained in Karachi without any formal accusation, and then released after strong pressure from the Italian government. The intelligence of my country were shown pictures of me with a Baloch representative in Europe, and on that ground, Pakistan attempted to accuse me of being an Indian spy. Following what could at best be described as a farcical detention, even my expulsion from the country turned into a bureaucratic comedy. The Federal Investigative Agency (FIA) struggled to deport me simply because it lacked the funds to cover the cost of my return ticket! I was ultimately granted an additional three days in Pakistan. However, my embassy told me to pack up and leave immediately, because they had credible intelligence that I would have "a car accident or be kidnapped by a terrorist" if I stayed any longer. The silver lining of these events was that since then, I have been considered more than reliable on matters pertaining to Pakistan, and am seen as a reference for all those opposing the Islamabad regime. That's how it started and that's why, when I started asking for information, the query reached the right people.

'I've been told you are looking for information about Balakot, madam. Is it correct?'

'Who told you?'

'Voices go around, madam. A friend said an Italian journalist was looking for somebody who knew something. But you see, nobody will talk; it is very dangerous. Only when he told me your name and I realised it was my old friend, I decided to call you. I still have your number, you see. And nobody knows I have it or that I know you.'

'Why are you willing to talk? As you said, it could be very dangerous.'

'Why are you asking? My daughter still talks about the foreign mama who treated and nursed her. And I know my old friend will never do something that could actually harm me. Besides, somebody has to tell the truth. You know what they are doing to us. You know the situation. Somebody has to talk.'

'Did you hear something? Some reliable voice?'

'No, madam. No voices. I was actually there.'

To say that I fell off my chair when I heard this, is an understatement. I could not believe it. I did not actually believe him until he told me the whole story, more than once. He narrated how and why he ended up there, and what had in the meantime happened to his family. For a second I thought he would or could frame me in some way, but then well, I had trusted him with my life once. And I still trusted him.

I called Praveen, and told him we had more than some information. We had an eyewitness.

This is the first article I wrote on the issue, titled: 'Eyewitnesses say IAF air strike in Balakot killed dozens of Jaish terrorists, a former ISI agent, ex-Pak army men', published on 2 March 2019 in the online magazine *Firstpost*:

> Eyewitnesses present at the site of India's 26 February bomb strikes against a Jaish-e-Muhammad base say they saw up to 35 bodies being transported out of the site by ambulance hours after the attack. The dead, they recounted, included 12 men who were said to have been sleeping in a single temporary

shack, and several individuals who had earlier served in Pakistan's military.

The sources, who work for local government authorities, declined to be identified as they are not authorised to speak to media, and said they feared reprisal. The eyewitnesses were contacted by this correspondent using encrypted communication.

"Local authorities reached the site soon after the bombing," one witness said, "but the area had already been cordoned off by then by the army, who did not even allow police to enter. The army also took away mobile phones from the medical staff on the ambulances."

A former Pakistani Inter-Services Intelligence (ISI) officer known locally as "Colonel Salim" was killed in the bombing, sources said, while a "Colonel Zarar Zakri" was injured. Mufti Moeen, a Jaish-e-Muhammad instructor from Peshawar, and improvised explosive device-fabrication expert Usman Ghani, were also killed in the bombing.

The largest single cluster of fatalities, the eyewitnesses said, were 12 Jaish-e-Muhammad fidayeen trainees, who were living in a single temporary earth-and-wood building that was flattened in the bombing.

Conflicting Testimony
Eyewitness testimony from the region has been conflicting, with witnesses variously saying there were no Jaish-e-Muhammad fighters at Jaba top, and others insisting they were present. The testimony has also been divided on whether

casualties were inflicted, with several local residents telling television and print journalists that the only victims were some civilians who received minor injuries.

However, the witnesses were only interviewed days after the attack, and several media outlets reported that they were not allowed unfettered access to all areas in Jaba, the village targeted in the raid.

Independent satellite imagery analysis conducted by Nathan Ruser of the prestigious Australian Strategic Policy Institute concluded that there is "no apparent evidence of more extensive damage and on the face of it does not validate Indian claims regarding the effect of the strikes".

However, Indian Air Force officials have asserted that that synthetic aperture radar—which provides finer spatial resolution than conventional beam-scanning radar—reveals that they destroyed four target buildings below the ridge, where the Jaish-e-Muhammad has several buildings, including a seminary.

The images, however, have not been made public, making it impossible to independently verify these claims.

Islamabad has said the Indian raid caused little damage, other than to local vegetation.

Indian intelligence sources said two of the names mentioned by the eyewitnesses—Usman and Colonel Salim—had also figured in communications intelligence available.

At an intelligence assessment meeting held on 1 March, India's Research and Analysis Wing (R&AW) said its communications intelligence could confirm five dead, but placed estimates of the killed in the region of 20.

R&AW had identified the Jaba top seminary as a target, based on intelligence that personnel earlier stationed by the Jaish-e-Muhammad at villages along the Line of Control had been pulled back to that location, in anticipation of possible Indian Army retaliation after the Pulwama suicide bombing.

"There's no doubt that bombs hit their targets," a senior intelligence official said. "Though some of the numbers that have been appearing in the media are hyperbolic, I think the raid served its purpose, which was to make a point about our ability to strike at terrorist safe-havens, rather than extract revenge." Some television channels reported that 300 people had been killed in the strike.

Past air strikes on terrorist targets have generally had a low deterrent effect, since the personnel at training facilities are generally small in the number and dispersed.

In 1998, the United States fired 75 cruise missiles at Al-Qaeda's Zhawar Kili in retaliation of the bombing at the American Embassies in Kenya and Tanzania in 1998, but killed only a dozen terrorists or less.

After the article was published, all hell broke loose.
Within a few hours, "Burnol" Ghafoor had managed to have a video released on social media. A video with pictures taken

from all over the web, in which I was basically accused of having written a book titled *Apocalypse Pakistan*, and of being associated with the former Pakistani Ambassador to the US, Husain Haqqani, and with Mehran Marri, former Baloch Representative to the UN. And, of course, of wearing a sari each time I travelled in India—undeniable proof, it seems, of being an Indian spy. Funnily enough, besides calling me a liar and a "paid" journalist (by the way, I don't know any journalist who actually works for free…) nobody countered the actual facts I had been stating.

I gave names and details in the article. It would have been quite simple to show on TV the people I had named, or to deny their existence. But no one, not even Major General "Burnol", bothered to do this. They chose instead to send after me on Twitter, a terrorist named Yahya Mujahid.

Mujahid, instead of discussing my Balakot source and the truth of my source's information, pulled up an old interview I had done with his boss, Mohammed Hafiz Saeed. According to Yahya, nobody could access His Holy Terror, but through him. As always, the claim was approximate at best. My interview is on record, and after a while, I threatened to reveal the name of the person who facilitated the meeting. A name they would definitely prefer remained private.

One of Burnol's trolls might have done a background check, because the harassment abruptly stopped.

However, all this only gave me a further confirmation of Asif's story.

Why should the ISPR chief take all that effort to discredit me if I had not struck a raw nerve? I knew I was inviting further trouble, but I wanted to dig deeper. That first conversation with Asif was hurried, and very cautious. I clearly told him to tell me only what he had personally seen and heard. He gave me a description of the scene, a very graphic one I must say. He gave me names, the same names I gave in my article, and which Praveen and I independently verified before going to print. This is how the conversation started:

> Mufti Asgar had reached there by six. Balakot is a one-and-a-half-hour journey... When he came to know about the attack... The attack was confirmed to him only after about half an hour or twenty minutes after the incident... He left his location... and reached there by six in the morning... He also remained in contact... The army reached there by 06:30. There is no army camp in Balakot... They are at Batrasi... By the time they could come from Batrasi... Since large vehicles could not come, so the army came in small vehicles... The army left their vehicles on the road below and then went up. At around 3-3:30, the aircraft had arrived... The search team was also with the army who searched all the area... Then a discussion took place... They instructed everyone not to make any noise otherwise Pakistan would be under pressure from the entire world. Then a team was constituted and it was decided that three persons from the tanzeem (JeM) would visit the family members of those who were killed and hand over the cash. Since the matter concerned the reputation of Pakistan, if it came out in the open, there would be a huge furore.

A book written three years later by the Indian Navy veteran Manan Bhatt, confirms Asif's words:

> The strikes shook up the entire Pakistan Military. They held an urgent meeting between the Pakistan Army Chief Qamar Javed Bajwa, Air Force Chief Marshal Mujahid Anwar Khan, and the head of the ISI, Lt Gen Asim Munir. The angered Army Chief had said, "Dobara hamari nak kat kar le gaye."

(For the second time, India has made us to eat the humble pie.) He ordered the PAF chief to carry out retaliatory action by the next day. Bajwa said, "Gen Munir (ISI chief), I want clearance of the debris from the seminary. I am giving you fifteen days. The markaz must look a madrassa only. Indians will soon share the videos of the strikes. Their actions will dent Pakistan's image internationally. India wants us to be designated as the state sponsor of terror."

"General Ghafoor, unlike 2016, this time, I want you to lead the way and take the attack to the enemy. You know what to do. Tell the world that they couldn't strike us. Show them that Markaz Syed Ahmed Shaheed is just a madrassa," Bajwa added.

But this, as I said, was almost three years later. At that moment, I did not have any other source, but Asif's account. All the "evidences" to the contrary shown by Pakistan and by the international media, basically confirmed the Pakistani version of the story.

Far too many questions lingered, were being asked and not answered.

Asif had told me he saw that night, 35 bodies being taken out by ambulances. Indian channels were reporting more than 300 casualties. But where were the bodies? And the wounded?

The site had been immediately cordoned off by the Army and nobody was allowed to go close to it. But why were the satellite images not showing any damage?

I sent a message to Asif, asking him to call when he could.

I needed answers.

And, I must say, I got more than what I was actually asking for.

DRAWING MAPS

'Are you sure you want to do this, madam?' asked Asif.

No, I wasn't really sure.

By then, I was already exhausted with this story, and fed up of being attacked both by Pakistani and Indian media, who were calling me "Modi cheerleader": forgetting I am not Indian, I don't vote in India, and frankly I cannot care less for who governs India. Or any other country, for that matter. What made it worse was watching even friends publicly undermine me on social media, not to debate the substance of my reporting, but to posture. They were eager to showcase their methodological superiority—declaring that nothing is credible unless confirmed by at least three independent sources and, ideally, also the blessing of God. Unsurprisingly, using that gold standard, they had found no "credible" evidence.

My source was the only direct one I had. The confirmations I received were indirect, and as is often the case in sensitive reporting—from individuals who could not be quoted.

Still, I am a journalist. I had a scoop, and decided to move forward.

By then, Asif had been able to gather more information, more precise intel.

The impact of the strike had immediately killed a large number of JeM cadre, he told me. 'At least 160-170 persons were killed on the spot.' Those killed included eleven trainers, ranging from bomb makers to those imparting weapons training. Two of these trainers were from Afghanistan. To prevent news on the fatalities from leaking through statements of family members of the cadre, a group of JeM members visited the families of those killed, and handed over cash compensation to them.

'Seventy-ninety persons were injured, some of them with very serious wounds.'

An Army unit from their camp in Shinkiari, arrived at the location of the strike at around 6 am, two-and-a-half hours later. Shinkiari is around 20 km away from Balakot, and the Army unit would have taken around 35–40 minutes to reach the location from where the climb to the camp begins. Incidentally, Shinkiari is also a base of the Pakistani Army, with the Junior Leaders Academy (JLA) located there.

Immediately after the Army unit's arrival, the injured were taken to a Harkat-ul-Mujahideen camp located in Shinkiari, and treated by Pakistani Army doctors. Asif told me:

> They took them there. The injured were taken there. They were given treatment by the Army which came from the Batrasi Camp in Mansehra. So, they were taken there... where they were provided treatment... roughly 15–20 persons died there. They had injuries on their arms, head or legs and were serious... 20–25 died later and among them were those who were injured in the head, neck, hips, limbs... do you understand... those who were very seriously injured... do you understand... later, when the day passed... then only those

were taken away... Later at night... their Army vehicles came and brought their equipment... then some people loaded the rubble in the vehicle... the lights of the vehicles were switched off... All lights were off. There is river Kunhar at Balakot. All the rubble was dumped in the river Kunhar.

He went on to add:
Cleaning of the area was done immediately... media was not allowed. Later, a shelter type structure was constructed at the site. They used old/used material for the shelter... later, the same was shown to the media. The media was told that it was a residential area and there was only a mosque present in the area for namaz and education for children. With this, there are 2–3 small rooms where 10- to 12-year-old children get education. These children are getting education for becoming Hafiz. At the side, there was the area for training where "mujahids" used to train... approximately eleven "ustads" were killed. Among them two were "barood masters" (explosive experts), another two used to deliver "khitab" (sermon) after the Roll Call to brainwash.

'Call to brainwash?' I asked.
Asif laughed:
Let me explain to you. After the morning namaz, they would "fall in" (fall in line) and then half an hour to a quarter of an hour would be spent on brainwashing by them... then at noon and in the evening. Rest of those who were teaching to handle Kalashnikov are gone... they were learning to shoot in the jungle... some were learning to make hideouts... they were killed. All of them in total make eleven. One of them was an Afghani... yes... one of those who used to train... So eleven "ustads" are among the 170. Then the Army took control of everything. Did

everything... including the cleaning of the debris. The remaining mujahids were told not to take any photograph/video or send them outside. Those who leak information outside would be killed along with their family members.

Interestingly enough, three years later, Manan Bhatt, gave an eyewitness account of those days. And, the account perfectly matches what Asif had told me between the end of February and the beginning of March 2019:

Despite the cessation of mobile network and media blackout, eyewitness accounts from people working in nearby hotels, and villagers from Bisian village, lay threadbare the entire chain of events. The strikes shook the whole Balakot Tehsil of Mansehra district in Khyber Pakhtunkhwa province of Pakistan. Villagers from Bisian and other eyewitnesses vividly remembered the effects of air strikes as equal to that of 5 Richter scale earthquakes as the earth shook each time a missile hit its target. GHQ rushed Pakistan Army to the scene of attack and dispatched columns from a nearby military unit for relief and rescue operations of JeM leadership and the cadre. Their priority remained the multi-story residential bungalow of Yusuf Azhar. But, by the time they reached, there was nothing left of him. The IAF strikes had eliminated Markaz Taleem-ul-Quran's training head without a trace. As [the] Pak Army reached the dormitories housing the terrorists, it was daylight, and the scenes in front of them were gruesome. The floors of buildings housing the terrorists had collapsed from within. [The] Army covered up the evidence of spice bombs entry in the large dormitory building by replacing the ruptured corrugated sheets with new ones. Disfigured bloodied corpses of those who got stuck below the debris looked as if army men [had] extracted them from their graves. In the night's dead, terror had arrived from thin air to strike those who sought to rain terror on innocent Indians. They shifted the scant few surviving terrorists to a nearby military hospital in an army ambulance. [The] next task was to remove the corpses stuck in the debris. Bodies kept on coming as they loaded them in private tempos, trailers, and military trucks, and took them for burial. Initially, they took care while picking up and loading the burnt bodies into trucks. But as the death toll mounted, they snatched two-three bodies at a time, and hurled them one over another inside the vehicles. It looked despicable as hands and feet of dead terrorists looked like sagged pendulums, necks drooped from shoulders. A few of the bodies were without heads as white bones protruded out of the neck cavity. Most of them looked burned and smashed. The soldiers had brought large black coloured polythene bags and were collecting bloodstained chopped body parts, spread over. Hijab clad women folk in Bisian village, talk in hushed voices of a mass burial site near FWO (Frontier Works Organization) staging post belonging to Army's 491 Engineer Group on Mansehra-Chilas Road. More than the corpses, removal of debris from the forested and mountainous regions remained an enormous task.

Asif had added something more:
They have kept 2–3 Qaris who are locals from Balakot and the remaining have been removed from there. From now on, if any media comes here they will only find small children taking education there. They have also brought more children from other madrasas. Apart from the 4 Qaris, there are 2–4 others who teach the children. The others believe that army is camped there, commanded by a Captain who is from Rawalakot. He is from Mujahid Battalion.

Adjacent to the Blue Pine Hotel located at the foothills from where one starts the trek for the JeM camp, Asif explained:

> There is now a freshly painted signboard that indicates the presence of the Taleem-ul-Quran on the hilltop. Unlike the earlier board, all links to the JeM leader and now internationally proscribed terrorist Masood Azhar, have been removed. The access to the dust track leading to the camp continued to be restricted, even to the local police. Apart from a few children and 3–4 teachers, the camp has been cleared of any traces of it earlier being a JeM camp.

Once again, Asif proved to be right.

On 10 April 2019, which is forty-two days after the Indian Air Force strike on Balakot, Pakistani authorities organised a visit of foreign media and defence attaches of foreign missions in the country, to the site.

Pakistani officials briefed the media that the site, which India had claimed to be a Jaish training camp, was actually an Islamic school, Taleem-ul-Quran madrasa for children, and this property had faced no damage in the so-called strikes by the Indian Air Force.

As per media reports, the visitors had to walk for an hour and a half uphill to reach the madrasa. On reaching the location, they were shown one large building that showed no signs of damage. There were around 200 students in the school. A few media reports were accompanied by photographs, showing students attending a class. One photo was of the exterior of the building where these classes were being held.

The visit lasted twenty minutes. Journalists and diplomats were allowed to freely interview the children and the teachers there, under the tender vigilance of the ISI.

According to the BBC report:
Foreign journalists and diplomats were taken by the Pakistani army on the visit to Balakot in Khyber Pakhtunkhwa state. They were shown a medium-sized crater which the army said had been made by an Indian air force bomb. A single house had been slightly damaged by the blast and a man had been injured,' the BBC's Usman Zahid reports. 'The visitors also saw some fallen trees. They were then taken to the Taleem ul Quran madrassa, the first such visit by foreign media. The large hilltop building is said to have a capacity for 2,500 children. Pakistani army spokesman Maj-Gen Asif Ghafoor insisted the madrassa did "no harm" and that Indian allegations that it was a terror training camp had "no truth". Some 150-200 children could be seen reciting the Koran in a mosque at the school. However, a teacher and a student interviewed by the BBC said they were all local people and that the madrassa had been shut since the Indian attack. While the media were allowed to take interviews they were told to keep them short and it was clear that the tour was being restricted.

As per the Al Jazeera report on 11 April:
An Al Jazeera visit to the site of the air raids a day after the attack found four distinct bomb craters on a forested mountainside, with little evidence of other damage. Interviews with residents, witnesses, local officials and medical personnel offered no evidence of mass casualties, as the Indian government had claimed. Residents and witnesses told Al Jazeera at the time that there was a religious school close to the targeted site, but that it was undamaged in the attack. A road sign for the school said that it was led by JeM Chief Masood Azhar and administered by Muhammad Yousaf Azhar, the JeM chief's brother-in-law. The

sign has since been removed, and journalists on Wednesday's military tour said it was no longer present. In the first-ever visit to the site of the school, journalists and diplomats were shown a large room where children were rocking back and forth as they read the Quran, and a set of buildings that appeared to be undamaged. Journalists who were on the trip told Al Jazeera on condition of anonymity. "It was difficult to be conclusive," said one reporter, pointing out how military personnel monitored the group throughout the delegation's visit and sometimes intervened during interviews with teachers and students. "The buildings did not look tampered with–the roofs didn't look new, everything there looked pretty old," the reporter said when asked if there appeared to be any evidence of the buildings having been repaired in the 43 days since the air raids. A second journalist who was on the tour corroborated that account. The journalists said there were between 75 and 100 students present at the school, and that most appeared to live in on-site dormitories, which the delegation was denied access to. Teachers at the school denied any links to JeM, the journalists said.

However, Asif maintained that a close comparison of the few images of the recent Pakistani Army sponsored excursion, and photos taken in 2018 of the Jaish camp in Balakot, clearly indicated that the visitors were indeed taken to the wrong location.

To understand what really had happened, I needed a clearer view of the site. What follows in the next paragraph is the exact transcription of a number of conversations I had on the issue with Asif. I even asked him to draw me a map and to describe exactly how the camp looked like before the strike. Asif went a step further, sending me pictures of the camp taken a year before, or in some cases, a few months before. In the pictures, you could clearly see all the JeM signs, and all that had changed after the strike.

In Asif's words:
Prior to entry into the above said centre, one has to cross through JeM's centre "Madrassa Taleem ul Quran" located on south-west of "Jaba-Bisian" road. From Bus Stand Mansehra, one has to take public transport, Suzuki Bolan vehicles, to reach the general area "Jaba" located on the Mansehra-Balakot Road, which takes around thirty minutes to cover the distance of around 18 km. A "Blue Pine Restaurant" is located near the "Bolan" stand, Jaba. One has to move on a "kucha" track towards the left side of the restaurant. On the other side of Blue Pine Restaurant, there is a sign board in Urdu indicating the direction towards Balakot Markaz of JeM, reading "Madrassa Taleem ul Quran, Balakot Road, Jaba, Mansehra". There is tough terrain or a steep kucha track from Blue Pine Restaurant point, towards JeM's Balakot Markaz. The total track is around three kilometres, and it takes around one hour to reach the main gate of the markaz on foot. The whole track is kucha, steep, and can be covered using medium-high powered motorcycles.

The complex that is spread out over 2 km, has a residence for trainers, a mosque, dormitory for mujahideen, a large open ground for outdoor activities, etc. At the main entrance of the markaz, there is a government security official making entries of all the visitors entering the facility. On one side of the entrance is the sign "Jaish-e-Muhammad", and on the other side the signboard "No Photography/Videography", written in the Urdu language. There is a small complex comprising a mosque, a kitchen and one room just inside the main entrance. On the right hand side of the entrance (back towards the main gate), there is an animal farm where rabbits and birds are kept. Armed JeM security personnel are deployed at the main gate. After moving around ten minutes south west of the main entrance, on the left hand side of the track, there is a small, single storey house around 25 yards away from the said track, where Ustaad Ghouri lives with his family members. After moving around 20 minutes further west, there is a small house (two rooms) on a hilltop, being used as residential accommodation by another senior Ustad (trainer) of the markaz.

Around 10 metres ahead of the previous location, the area of the main markaz starts. There is a security barrier using bamboo, where a JeM cadre performs duty as security in-charge. On the right hand side of the said barrier, vegetable plantation and a small chicken house is visible. After moving five minutes further south west, the main mosque of the markaz appears. There is a huge mosque with a large prayer hall, five rooms, a courtyard, a big kitchen and four bathrooms. On the back side (west) of the mosque, there is vast open plantation area. The main madrassa of the markaz is also located inside the mosque, which accommodates around 250 students. These students are imparted religious/jehadi training (non-military) in different courses being conducted inside the markaz.

An iron (meshed wire) gate is located at a distance of 200 metres from the main mosque of the markaz. Thereafter, there is a large playground/assembly/open activity area for cadre. On the left side of the ground, there is a small complex comprising a kitchen, two rooms and a washroom. Near that ground, there is a medium-sized "Woodcutter Machine" (Aara) being used to cut wood for construction activities inside the markaz. A small mosque is located nearby.

Just ahead of that mosque, there exists a two-storey building. The ground floor of the said building (two-room set) is being used as the residence of Maulana Yousuf Azhar, the person in-charge of Balakot Markaz. The first floor is being used as residential accommodation for other teachers or trainers of the markaz.

Also, there is a well-equipped guesthouse on the first floor of the markaz. Adjacent to that building (residence of Yousuf Azhar), there is a small canteen. Just 50 metres ahead of the canteen, there is another guesthouse (two rooms) for common functionaries visiting the markaz from outside. Also, there is a kitchen for students and a big hall (about 75' x 75'), which is being used as accommodation for under-training "mujahideen".

Cadre of JeM were imparted military training in batches of 30–35 each inside Balakot Markaz. There is a deep gorge at the back side of the above-mentioned large hall (accommodation of "mujahideen"). There is another zig-zag road leading from Maulana Yousuf Azhar's residence towards a spring. Adjacent to Maulana Yousuf Azhar's residence, there are two huge water tanks to store water being brought by cadre from the spring. There is a check post just ahead of the above-mentioned spring, being manned by two armed JeM cadre round the clock.
Ahead of this point is a "No Entry" area for all, other than the cadre attaining military training, their trainers and senior JeM functionaries. The main training area/firing range/demolition

activities ground is located ahead of this check post at a distance of around one hour (on foot), i.e., around three kilometres. This area is known as Khyber Point.

The building that was shown to the diplomats and journalists, is marked as the "Hall" in the illustration of the terror camp site drawn for me by Asif. This hall was being used to provide training in Islamic theology to the younger students, who were still in the initial stages of their training. However, it is unlikely that the visitors were taken to the rear side of the camp where the mujahids lived and underwent their military training.

Photos dating to 2018 of the exterior of the "Hall" that I have in my possession, and the latest taken by the visiting journalists, clearly show that the building has been spruced up and possibly given a fresh coat of paint.

Another notable change was the addition of a new green board hoisted at the entrance of the hall. Further, old photos of the inside of the hall have flags of JeM, and posters of the terror group all over the walls. The recent photos show clean, bare walls devoid of any posters or flags.

There was no doubt in my mind—the camp had undergone significant renovation in the last few weeks. This would explain why Pakistani authorities took more than a month to unveil what they presented as a children's madrasa to the world. A madrasa, which rather than being located close to inhabited areas, was built on a remote hilltop, requiring its young students to undertake a few hours of uphill trekking.

Sources located in the Balakot area have maintained that the Pakistan Army is still in control of the hilltop, with locals not being allowed access.

If the site was indeed a madrasa, why was the Pakistan Army

stationed there, and treating it as a restricted area?

One of my sources who travelled to the Blue Pine Hotel at the foothills of the camp site, sent a photo of the new signboard of the Taleem-ul-Quran madrasa, which had replaced the earlier board that had clearly declared Masood Azhar's links to the madrasa. The new signboard makes no such claims.

As Pakistan continues to try and whitewash its links to terror groups, it exposes its reluctance to take credible steps against this hydra-headed monster of Islamic terror groups that it has created. The choice of the site was not casual, not for JeM, not for the Indian Army.

The place is in fact, first of all, a powerful symbol.

Jaish-e-Mohammad (JeM) purposefully chose Balakot for establishing its training centre, after its formation in early 2000. The location has a highly symbolic and strategic value for the jihadi narrative and its operations.

Situated on the banks of the river Kunhar at a distance of nearly 18 miles from the city of Mansehra in Khyber Pakhtunkhwa, Pakistan, Balakot is the place where Syed Ahmad Barelvi (1786–1831) of Rae Bareli (now in Uttar Pradesh, India) and Shah Ismail (1779–1831), waged "jihad" against the Sikh kingdom of Maharaja Ranjit Singh, and were killed in battle on 6 May 1831. Balakot is also the gateway to the Kaghan Valley.

Historians claim that Balakot has remained in many ways the "epicentre of jihad in South Asia". Syed Ahmad Barelvi, an Islamist cleric from Rae Bareli, after spending two years in Arabia, returned with a mission that combined Wahabi intolerance and jihadist zeal. In a short time, he became immensely popular among North Indian Muslims. Soon after his return, he declared jihad against the "infidel" Sikh empire. He and his followers arrived in the Peshawar Valley, demanding that the Pathan tribesmen renounce their tribal customs and accept the Sharia. However, this did not hold much appeal to the Pathans. From 1826, Barelvi and his band of Ghazis waged many skirmishes against the Khalsa army. The final decisive battle was fought in May 1831.

Sher Singh, a commander under Maharaja Ranjit Singh, led Sikh forces that lay in wait for the "mujahideen" in Muzaffarabad, not far from Balakot. On 6 May 1831, in a battle that lasted most of the day, amidst war cries of "Allah-o-Akbar" and "Wahe Guruji di Fateh", Syed Ahmed and Shah Ismail were killed, along with many of their "mujahideen".

Balakot's association with the idea and practice of jihad in South Asia was reinforced in the 1990s, when terrorist groups set up training camps in its environs, to prepare for their campaign against the Indian security forces stationed in Jammu and Kashmir. For these terrorists, Syed Ahmad and Shah Ismail are revered heroes, whose jihad they aspire to emulate. Syed Ahmad is portrayed as an early figure attempting to establish an Islamic state governed by strict enforcement of Islamic law. A mazar of Syed Ahmad still exists in Balakot. Owing to the significance attached to the initiation of jihad in South Asia at this place, JeM, with the active support of the Afghan Taliban and the Pakistan Intelligence Agency, established this training camp for its mujahideen for terror operations in India, and to complement the Afghan Taliban in their Afghanistan operations.

It has also come to notice that Al Qaida operatives may also have been trained in JeM's Balakot camp. In fact, US authorities became aware of this through the arrest of some operatives linked to the camp, highlighting the cross-group use of militant facilities in the region.

A 2004 United States Department of Defence interrogation report stated that Balakot had "a training camp that offers both basic and advanced terrorist training on explosives and artillery". In contrast, military analysts asserted that whilst the area used to host militant camps, they dispersed after the 2005 Pakistan earthquake to avoid detection by the international aid groups providing relief in the area. *The New York Times* reported that western security officials had doubts about the existence of such large-scale training camps, asserting that Pakistan no longer runs them and that "militant groups are spread out in small groups around the country", while Reuters quoted locals saying that the camp (or the children's school) had been shut down a year before. According to intelligence sources, it was a fully-operational JeM training camp:

Since its inception, cadres trained at this centre continue to be sent to both Afghanistan and J&K in India for attacks. Cadres who have successfully completed all basic Jihadi courses at Markaz Usman-o-Ali, Bahawalpur or other markaz/madrasas of JeM, are considered for military/jihadi training in Balakot Markaz. A number of events like debate competitions (Jihadi and Military type), physical exercise completion, passing out parade, are organised routinely at this markaz attended by senior JeM functionaries. Each batch consists of 30–50 students including Afghan mujahideen.

At that point, however, half of the world of social media had turned into a world of military experts. Analyses had been commissioned to a number of think-tanks around the planet, to show with satellite images, how the buildings were intact, and those analyses were hugely advertised on media and social media.

However, let's dig deeply into this and listen to the story from another perspective. The perspective of the person who actually commanded the operation.

OF WALLS AND ENEMIES

I had an interview with former Indian Air Chief Marshal BS Dhanoa.

'There are two things. One is winning the perception battle and the second is winning the military battle. Unfortunately, we did not consider the perception battle so much,' replied Air Force Chief BS Dhanoa to one of my questions.

However, let us go back to what we were talking about, and to the long conversation Dhanoa and I had about the Balakot operation, in which he clarified *a posteriori*, all the doubts one could still have.

Let me do a quick though not-so exhaustive recap of what happened post the Balakot strike. India confirmed they hit the target, but did not release any images of the attack, stating that it was classified information. A few days later, the Indian Air Force shared high-resolution satellite images with media outlets such as *India Today*. These photographs showed what appeared to be "holes" in the roofs of some buildings—damage analysts described as "a classic signature of SPICE bombs", precision-guided munitions known for their effectiveness against hardened targets.

According to Indian officials, the roofs of some buildings made of corrugated galvanised iron (CGI) sheets were missing, and were quickly replaced two days later.

As I had mentioned earlier, after a short panicked moment, Pakistan went into full denial mode. Balakot was a religious school, Indians did not hit any target except crows and trees, which were promptly shown on air by journalist Hamid Mir as I had mentioned earlier. Media outlets, both local and foreign, were denied access to the area, but they could instead freely interview terrified villagers presented as "neutral sources".

It is also important to note that these interviews were conducted for the international press by local stringers. Locals, hence vulnerable to threats or blackmail, especially in a place like Pakistan. But strangely enough, nobody ever questioned the reliability and freedom of their reporting.

The reality is that no independent assessment was possible or allowed by Pakistan. But despite this lack of access and transparency, the Pakistani narrative began to be adopted by a good number of international think-tanks and media outlets, without thorough verification or room for doubt. The entire narrative quickly shifted towards demanding proof from India. But even when India provided satellite imagery and technical assessments, these were either downplayed or dismissed by the same outlets that had unquestioningly accepted Pakistan's claims.

This glaring disparity in standards of credibility is not unique. Two years later, the Taliban, going their masters' way, were denying the death of Al Qaida leader Ayman al-Zawahiri, in a US drone strike in Kabul saying "there are no evidences" he was in Kabul or that he died in the American attack. But nobody took them seriously or even bothered to report the news, because no one questions America. Apparently, the Taliban are not to be trusted, and rightly so. Yet Pakistan, a country with a long history of lies and deceit and of creating and harbouring terrorists, must be believed at face value. This selective scrutiny is not only intellectually dishonest, but also dangerously distorting. It allows State actors with opaque records and strategic interests in fostering militancy to dominate the narrative, while other countries are held to near-impossible standards.

'What the international press was looking from us was a briefing in which we declassify it (Balakot) and the pictures,' commented Dhanoa. 'I will show you this picture of American attacks on this so-called Syrian biological weapon. You will see such small-small holes, but that they said was good, they said they had been able to hit.'

And yet, nobody ever questioned or asked for proof from the Americans.

'There were basically two problems,' added the former Air Force Chief. 'The first one being that the international press does not take off-the-record briefings, while the Indian press took off-the-record briefings. The second, is a technical one: you never part with your capability till you stop using it. During the Kargil War, we kept classified what we were doing, but when we got the Sukhoi 30 in numbers, we got the MiG-21 in numbers, then we said, okay, this is how we did it in Kargil because we no longer used that system. As long as we are using that system, that particular method of attack, things like that cannot be declassified just to win a propaganda battle.'

This approach underscores a broader military doctrine: operational details are safeguarded until their disclosure no longer poses a risk to current or future missions. The IAF's decision to withhold certain information, even at the expense of immediate public relations benefits, reflects a commitment to long-term strategic security over short-term narrative control.

But the propaganda battle was, without any doubt, won by Pakistan.

For days, both social and official media were full of satellite data analysis showing how and why India missed the target.

The Australian Strategic Policy Institute research, analysing the main building, concluded that, there was '*...no apparent evidence of more extensive damage and on the face of it does not validate India's claims regarding the effect of the strike*', adding that the missiles missed the targets because of a "systematic targeting error". Michael Sheldon of the Atlantic Council who was investigating the issue, concluded that something appeared to have gone wrong in the targeting process, and that no damage was inflicted to the structures of the site.

Reuters went further, analysing Planet Labs' high resolution satellite images, and showing how compared to the same images taken in 2018: '*There were no discernible holes in the roofs of buildings, no signs of scorching, blown-out walls, displaced trees around the madrasa or other signs of an aerial attack.*'

European Space Imaging also provided high resolution images of the site, the day after the attack: '*There were no signs of scorching, no large distinguishable holes in the buildings and no signs of stress to the surrounding vegetation.*'

However, according to the former Air Force Chief, they showed '*...the wrong buildings intact!*'

So once again, let's start from the beginning: Pulwama. Former Indian Air Chief Marshal BS Dhanoa stated: '*14 February 2019. Valentine's Day. I had just returned from Bangladesh and I told my guys that this is coming to us because too many people had died. And I knew after the Uri strikes, they would have removed their people from the forward launch hubs. So I told my people this is coming to us. So we were prepared.*'

How was the preparation done?
Former Indian Air Chief Marshal BS Dhanoa:
Let me go way back, when I was Wing Commander and the Parliament attack happened. Even then, well before that, when the Jammu and Kashmir Assembly attack happened, we knew we needed to prepare and make plans. So when the Parliament attack happened on 13 December 2001, we were ready. Yes, we were ready even then. See, identification of terrorist camps is the job of Intelligence, and it takes time. From my point of view, I can tell you there are buildings A, B, C or D. I can tell you what the buildings are made of, but I have no idea of who is inside the buildings. That's Intelligence's job, and as I said, it takes time. So, to go back to your question, it is not that we suddenly got ready after Pulwama happened. We had been ready for a long time. But you know, to launch a strike is a political decision, not a military one. After Pulwama, we had been given the "go ahead".

How and why was the target chosen?
It was a Jaish-e-Mohammed camp, first of all. We were told that a large number of people were there, ready to cross the LoC. Besides this, we knew that other than the kids studying at the madrassa, there were none or very few civilians around. We made sure not to damage those [civilian] spots.

How many planes were sent?
Sorry, but that information is still classified. Because, you see, there is a full system at stake. It is not only the people who are delivering the bombs, there are a lot of people carrying out electronic warfare, a lot of people carrying out the air defence, a lot of people carrying out air surveillance. Plus, we

must also remember the famous strike the British did on the Falklands and Port Stanley in 1982. They dropped eighteen bombs on the Vulcan, when only one was the target. But there is something known as over target requirement. So, you cater for that, and you have to cater for failures also.... After all, everything is mechanical, so with that, we had enough to do the required damage that we needed done, and the number of buildings we were supposed to hit.

The number of bombs is classified too, I guess?
No, the number of bombs which hit, we are talking of five to eight bombs.

But Pakistan continues to deny that you hit the target. All the international OSINT analyses showed the buildings intact.
The wrong buildings were intact. The type of weapon makes a lot of difference. But the question is, since when were you prepared. We have been prepared for a very long time. All terrorist camps are not in Balakot. Many of them are in Muzaffarabad. Even if we hit Muzaffarabad, we don't want to kill civilians. It gets very bad press and everything goes wrong. We are not a super power like America.

Meaning, the Americans can kill civilians as "collateral damage" and get away with it?
The weapon we chose is one which has maximum shrapnel and lower blast. You see, when you go against the Army, you want to flatten everything. So you go with weapons which have higher explosive content. Basically, to hit the target, you want the bomb to explode in a cavity. Suppose you have a

building, ideally, the bomb should break through the roof and explode inside.

You are talking of the SPICE bombs, right?
Yes. They explode in a cavity, and when they explode, everybody in the cavity will go. When a bomb explodes on the roof, the roof will fall in. But suppose I am under a table, nothing will happen to me. Or, I am lucky to be in a corner, I am probably not going to be hit. That's why we went for using a special weapon, where you adjust the fuse. You know how thick the concrete is, what the strength of the concrete is. So you keep the explosion delay until it breaks. In this case, it hit the floor and only then it exploded. So, the buildings are still intact, but the entry holes are clearly visible even in commercial satellite imagery.

Yet, nobody believes you did it!
Let me get this straight—my goal was to hit Jaish-e-Mohammed, to convey a message to them, not to convince the international press. I did not think of propaganda. My primary goal was to convey a message to Jaish-e-Mohammed. No matter where you are, if you carry a terror strike inside India, we will get you. And I think that the message was conveyed. They got it. Because since then, there has not been a single major terrorist attack. As I said, my primary goal was to kill terrorists, to send a clear message to them. Not to convince the international press or to show the world that India could retaliate and do something. Otherwise, there are lots of other things we could have done.

So, you wanted to hit the JeM?
Yes, to tell them what they do comes at a cost. The weapon was chosen to kill more terrorists. In any weapon, some will fail. You see how many missiles they fired in the Tomahawk missile, when Clinton struck bin Laden. Sixty-six missiles they had fired and bin Laden was still alive. In August 2002, in Pakistan, there was an incident I recall. It was on the Line of Control, from where they keep firing all the time. They had established a new post. We sent four Mirages, dropped lots of bombs in the area. They left and never came back. They got the message. And if now you ask me a technical question, did all the four Mirages hit, the answer is no. That is why we have redundancy, that is why we have something called the "over the target requirement". That is why when we require one, we send four. In any battle planning, it is done like that. If the target is of importance, they say in statistics, one sigma is 70 per cent and two sigma is 95 per cent.

So, the crows and trees were killed by the over the target requirements?
No, no, this is not the kind of bomb that kills trees and crows. I guess that when they realized that this had happened, they created surface exposures through IEDs. In that moment, they did not know which bomb we had used. The bomb that we have used would have dug a hole, it would not have created that kind of surface exposure, the way that they are depicting. The trees and crows they are showing you, have been hit in an IED type of explosion, a surface explosion, which they have done just to show that we have missed them. Moreover, if the bombs had missed the target, they would have had some components of the bomb. The entire bomb does not vanish

into thin air. They would have shown those components. They could not, because they don't have them.

The Washington Post attempted a political analysis of the issue: "...these latest details about the India-Pakistan air battles threaten to discredit the BJP narrative and undermine its electoral prospects. Open-source satellite imagery revealed India did not hit any targets of consequence in the airstrikes it conducted, after the terrorist attack on the paramilitaries. Additionally, reporting indicates that during the February 27 air battle, friendly fire from an air-defence missile brought down an Indian military helicopter, killing six military personnel."

Former Indian Air Chief Marshal BS Dhanoa:
Well, the DG ISPR (Director General, Inter-Services Public Relations Pakistan) first said they did not use an F16, then they said yes we did, then claimed they got two [Indian] pilots, then the pilot became one. You cannot really go by what they claim. They also claimed that the Balakot camp was a madrassa, a religious school for children.

Yes. A school set, according to my sources, more than an hour's walk from any surrounding village....
Obviously, the only reason to set a camp there is to keep onlookers away. But then yes, let us suppose it was indeed a school, a madrassa, whatever you want to call it. A school is not an atomic facility, everyone can go visit a school. So then why did they not allow anyone to go there for 42 days? If there was no damage, I, if in their place, would have taken the press there immediately to show them the truth. If we had not hit anything, they should have shown the place the day after.

Why did they not do it?
They were clearing up the area, that's why. Changing the covers on the roofs. And even then, after 42 days, they took the press only to the mosque. And the mosque, trust me, was never intended to be a target. We never intended to hit the children studying in the madrasa. It was not a kill-all mission. We are not Clint Eastwood (smiles). As I said, after 42 days, they could not manage to take the visitors near any other building because the damage inside was too big, and they were not able to fix it even after a month.

The Pakistani Army was taken completely by surprise?
Two hundred per cent. That was my aim. The first thing I said was that if we are not sure about the communication, we do not talk. Very few people knew about it. I conducted all operations as normal, and on that day, I was behind the Prime Minister when we inaugurated the National War Memorial. Later, I went to the mess, attended my CC's farewell, and we had a banquet. Even my wife did not know about it. She was surprised when I started getting calls in the morning.

In 2011, I had told former Pakistani President Musharraf, while talking of the Abbottabad operation, exactly this: 'God help you if India decides to do the same.' He had replied: 'Indians are not capable of doing it. They are not strong enough to do this and Pakistan will teach them a lesson if they ever try.'
They are more into emotions than facts. As usual, they cannot afford to lose the perception battle, especially with the Urdu press. Take Kargil. I fought in Kargil, flew a MiG-21. I was in Srinagar at that time, when they refused to take the bodies of their dead soldiers, claiming that they were not their people. We,

the Indian Army, buried them on a hilltop, with full religious procedures and military honours. They did not take the bodies back saying they were not theirs. But in his book, Musharraf said that they were actually their own people. So, I would have loved to ask him why he lied in 2002. Not taking your soldiers' bodies back for a ritual burial is something totally unheard of. But they did it. This is what they do. They backflip things when it suits them. Truth is, they are the Army of an impoverished country, and they have to sell to their people the story of the invincible Army standing between the country and the arch-enemy, preventing the country from being taken by India.

Summing up the story, what would you like to tell people?
The purpose of the Balakot strike, as I already said, was to tell Jaish-e-Mohammad that if you carry out terrorist attacks on Indian soil, whether you are in Pakistan-occupied Kashmir or you are in Pakistan, we will get you. And, they got the message loud and clear. We had no major terror strikes throughout the time of the Indian elections, even after Article 370 was revoked in Kashmir, and till I retired as the Chief of Air Staff. That was my goal and I achieved it. To convince the international press has never been my primary goal. Is it better to convince the international press or the Jaish-e-Mohammad?

***

Even if the JeM was convinced, the international press has always been far from being convinced. This, despite the open source intelligence (OSINT) analysis being made by retired Squadron Leader Samir Joshi, according to whom there are reasons why the satellite image analysis done by international think-tanks got the operation completely wrong.

First of all, according to Joshi, they all wrongly assumed that the main target was "the big white building", the mosque that was later shown to the international press, while the main target was not the mosque but the mujahid hostel.

Then, not knowing what kind of weapons had been used for the attack, they were all looking for evidence of a large explosion, and for a building that had been destroyed or had collapsed. The Indian Army used the Spice 2000 penetrator version. These are bombs that explode in a cavity without collapsing the building. They also assumed, according to Joshi, that India would have used the Standard SRTM Digital Elevation Model (Shuttle Radar Topography Mission DEM) data, which has a margin of error, and could possibly lead to a missed target. Moreover, all the foreign media assessment had been stating incorrect launch directions.

What the media had been shown forty-two days later was just the mosque. The mosque had been whitewashed and changed into a "normal" religious school. The picture of the place sent to me by Asif perfectly matched with this kind of narrative.

Until before the Balakot air strikes, the place was full of JeM flags and signboards. But they all vanished after the attack. Joshi analyses the F16 debate that followed the Balakot strike. It might be interesting to have a look at it. It might also be interesting to try and understand why news internationally has overwhelmingly carried only the Pakistani narrative on the incident.

One might argue that it has to do a lot with the usual, very well-known elephant in the room—the American fear of the nuclear bomb in Pakistan, and of the dire consequences of a full-blown war between India and Pakistan.

When Pulwama happened, all the countries rushed to present their condolences to India, adding invariably the recommendation to both countries to "exercise restraint". Restraint is something India has always exercised each time a terror attack from Pakistan took place. But there was criticism, a lot of criticism in the country, for the feeble response India gave to previous attacks—the Parliament attack in 2001 and the Mumbai attacks in 2008.

As Dhanoa noted, while cross-border military strikes may not lead to Pakistan dismantling its terror network, it would send a strong message that Pakistan's behaviour would incur consequences. From India's point of view, the Balakot strike also dispelled the notion that the use of airpower is escalatory, and that retaliation in response to terrorist acts would invariably lead to a full scale war. From its side, Pakistan continues to use the habitual recipe of blackmail and military pride, not so much against India, but threatening the rest of the world in a not-so veiled way, of the consequences of a war with India.

In February 2020, speaking at the International Institute for Strategic Studies-Centre for International Strategic Studies (IISS-CISS) workshop in London, retired Lt Gen Khalid Kidwai noted that Pakistan has a 'declared policy of "Quid Pro Quo Plus" against a limited Indian attack'. He added that 'Pakistan's nuclear weapons continue to serve the purpose for which they were developed,' and went on to say, 'It is precisely the presence of these nuclear weapons that deters, and in this specific case, deterred India from expanding operations beyond a single unsuccessful airstrike.'

'With neither side wanting to back down on its public posture, the graduated use of military force is likely in a future crisis,' writes Lt Gen Deependra Singh Hooda (Retd), adding that 'the "Quid Pro Quo Plus" strategy noted by Lt Gen Kidwai is an attempt by Pakistan to restore nuclear deterrence by claiming that Pakistan is willing to climb the escalation ladder. India sees this as a bluster. The point, at the end of the day, is not whether the Indian Air Force has hit the target, but what it openly, and, once for all, states is that since then, no terrorist attack will be tolerated anymore without a reply.

On my front, I noted a peculiar personal development after Balakot happened—I wrote articles after the attack, Ghafoor made that cute video on me—my name was struck off from the guest list of the Pakistani Embassy in Italy. And nobody from that embassy responds to my requests for comments or interviews on this and other matters, since then.

INDIA'S BRAIN

'India's brain is not working. They are trying to threaten us. But are their threats making us scared? Certainly not. In fact, their threats encourage us. Their threats do the same trick as public appreciation does for a poet reciting his poetry.'

It was 28 February, two days after Balakot, when Masood Azhar wrote these lines in his column in *Al Qalam*, under the *nom de plume* of Saadi. They were a message, not only to India, but to the Pakistani establishment as well. But let's first go back a couple of days. Let's go back to that 14 February, when half of the world (and all social media) where busy exchanging Valentine's Day greetings, and the other half was busy trashing those who indulged in this. When, amongst bunches of flowers, red, heart-shaped balloons, and cheesy sentences of eternal love and affection, the news literally deflagrated. A convoy of seventy-eight vehicles carrying more than 2,500 members of the Central Reserve Police Force, was attacked by a vehicle-borne suicide bomber. The convoy was travelling on the National Highway 44 from Jammu to Srinagar, and was hit at Lethampora, in the district of Pulwama. The attack was quite well-planned and the attackers well-informed.

The convoy had left Jammu around 3.30 early morning, and was carrying a large number of people because the highway had been shut down for two days before. At Lethampora, the convoy was rammed from behind by a car packed with explosives. It killed 40 personnel of the 76th Battalion and injured many more. The car was driven by 22-year-old Adil Ahmad Dar from Kakapora, a nearby tehsil in district Pulwama. The terror strike was however, claimed almost immediately by the infamous Pakistan-based terrorist group, Jaish-e-Mohammed, quite well-known in the subcontinent. They released a video of Dar, who had joined the group a year earlier. According to his family, he had left the house on a bicycle one fine day, and never returned. JeM leader Masood Azhar was back after a couple of years on all Indian and international media. In Italy, I had quite a difficult task for a specialist on the Indian subcontinent—explaining facts to a widely not really interested audience, an audience that had little or no knowledge at all of the background history. Therefore, it was quite difficult, to make people in Italy and Europe understand the matter—to make them understand why the outrage spread so widely and so deeply in India, why New Delhi immediately blamed Pakistan for the blast, and later, why Balakot happened.

Following the Pulwama attack, India accused Pakistan for allowing the JeM and other armed groups to operate freely on its soil, with one top Indian general going so far as to say that Pakistani intelligence had "controlled" the attack. Until then, the story was following a very well-known plot, the same plot followed after the Mumbai attack in 2008. That a Pakistani-based, ISI-controlled terror group carried out an attack in India, and that New Delhi formally accused Islamabad, and Islamabad in turn, asked for "reliable" evidences. When the evidences are provided, they would say these are not substantial and deny everything.

Meanwhile, just to show some degree of goodwill and to prove they are against terrorism, they would arrest a certain number of minor members of this or that terror organisation. This was also a pattern of behaviour successfully used for years with the Americans during the famous "war on terror". Musharraf, in his memoirs, gave several examples of it. The same Musharraf, who by the way, while talking to me in London, candidly labelled the Mumbai attack as a "RAW and ISI business, they are constantly at each other's throats".

All this aside, let's return to Pulwama and the dossier provided by India to Islamabad. On 27 February, India shared a dossier of evidences linked to the attack with Pakistan, days after Pakistani Prime Minister Imran Khan had invited Indian authorities to share "actionable intelligence" on the attack. The dossier contained "specific details" of the involvement of the Jaish-e-Mohammad (JeM) in the Pulwama terror attack on the CRPF, as also the presence of camps of the UN-proscribed terror outfit in the country. The Indian Ministry of External Affairs said Pakistan was informed that India expected Islamabad to take immediate and verifiable action against terrorism emanating from territories under its control. In response to the Indian counter-terror operation, the Pakistan Air Force tried to target certain locations in Jammu and Kashmir, which was countered by IAF jets. In the engagement, India shot down a Pakistani jet, while an Indian IAF pilot was captured by the Pakistani authorities. India also lost a MiG-21 aircraft.

India lodged a strong protest at the unprovoked act of aggression by Pakistan, including the violation of the Indian air space and the targeting of military posts. 'This is in contrast to India's non-military anti-terror pre-emptive strike at a JeM terrorist camp in Balakot on February 26,' the MEA added. As in the Balakot case, the riddle of lies, half-truths, fake news, and opinions that passed for news, went on for days. This time, it went further than what happened after Balakot. Ghafoor's troll factory was working 24x7, and Pakistan succeeded in gaining one of its "famous brilliant, successful victories"—the social media one. The Pulwama dossier, of course, ended up like the Mumbai one. Or the Abbottabad one, for all that it mattered. On 5 March, Pakistani authorities said they had detained forty-four members of various armed groups, including relatives of Jaish-e-Mohammad (JeM) chief Masood Azhar. The detainees included Abdul Rauf, Azhar's brother, and Hammad Azhar, the JeM chief's son. Both names were in the Indian dossier. However, on 27 March, the Pakistani Foreign Office stated that: '…while 54 detained individuals are being investigated, no details linking them to Pulwama have been found so far. Similarly, the 22 pin locations shared by India have been examined. No such camps exist. Pakistan is willing to allow visits, on request, to these locations.' Pakistan added that it remained "committed" to investigating the attack, and requested "additional information and documents" to continue the process. So, all was as it always had been. JeM claimed the attack, but according to Pakistan there were no "substantial" evidences. And all the training camps are, of course, resorts where children of terrorists spend their summer holidays.

I remember being given only 20 lines by *Limes—Italian Review of Geopolitics*, to comment on the Pulwama attack, explain why it happened, to say who Jaish-e-Mohammed was, and what they wanted. The Army of Mohammed, the Jaish, in Italy, means literally nothing for the majority of people. To make people understand, you have to start connecting dots, telling stories and evidencing links with names and organisations they are familiar with—Al Qaida, Taliban, ISIS. To make people understand, you have to go back to a very far away place, a place far in time and space. You have to go back to the beginning.

Go back to when little Masood was not sporting a beard yet, and was only the son of a Deobandi cleric in Bahawalpur, Pakistan. Dad was not a terrorist, but certainly was a fanatic religious extremist who made sure his son and all the rest of the family received the "right" kind of education. Azhar was inspired to jihad by his older brother Ibrahim Azhar, who fought in Afghanistan during the 1980s. It was he who took Masood in 1988 to Afghanistan. But unlike Ibrahim, Masood was not a fighter, but an ideologue and an inspiring orator. He graduated from the Jamia Ulum Islamic madrasa, an institution that was closely linked to the extremist organisation, Harkat-ul-Ansar (HuA), with its key ideology being supporting the proxy war against Indian forces in Kashmir. From there, he started his career. After he suffered injuries in the Soviet-Afghan War, Azhar was chosen as the head of Harkat's department of motivation. Azhar later became the General Secretary of Harkat-ul-Ansar, and visited many international locations to recruit, raise funds and spread the message of pan-Islamism. He travelled to the UK via Saudi Arabia in August 1993, visited various mosques in the UK and delivered lectures to youth on jihad. Special references were made to Afghanistan/Bosnia/Kashmir, where he said that Islam was "suppressed". He further instigated them to safeguard Islam by volunteering their services in the name of Allah.

This is how a BBC article describes his visit:

> When one of the world's most important jihadist leaders landed at Heathrow airport on 6 August 1993, a group of Islamic scholars from Britain's largest mosque network was there to welcome him. Within a few hours of his arrival he was giving the Friday sermon at Madina Mosque in Clapton, east London.

His speech on the duty of jihad apparently moved some of the congregation to tears. Next stop—according to a report of the jihadist leader's own magazine—was a reception with a group of Islamic scholars where there was a long discussion on "jihad, its need, training and other related issues".

The visiting preacher was Masood Azhar. According to BBC, after a series of speeches at east London mosques, Azhar headed north. Zakariya Mosque in Dewsbury, Madina Masjid in Batley, Jamia Masjid in Blackburn and Jamia Masjid in Burnley, were among the venues for his jihadi sermons in his first ten days in Britain. Azhar also gave a speech at an important Islamic institution in Britain—a boarding school and seminary in Lancashire known as Darul Uloom Bury. 'According to the report of the trip, Azhar addressed the students and teachers, telling them that a substantial proportion of the Quran had been devoted to "killing for the sake of Allah" and that a substantial volume of sayings of the Prophet Muhammad were on the issue of jihad…' the article goes on to say. Quoting Masood Azhar's words from a speech titled "From Jihad to Jannat", 'The youth should prepare for jihad without any delay. They should get jihadist training from wherever they can. We are also ready to offer our services.' And so he did.

Masood Azhar was finally arrested in Anantnag while visiting J&K, to coordinate the activities of the terror group, Harkat-ul-Jihad-al-Islami. HuA did its best to release Masood from Indian custody, including kidnapping foreign tourists while they were visiting Kashmir. He spent five years in jail. Indian investigators claim he told them, 'You people will not be able to keep me in custody for long. You don't know how important I am for Pakistan and the ISI. You are underestimating my popularity. The ISI will ensure that I am back in Pakistan.' But he was released, along with other two terrorists in exchange for hostages, only after an Indian Airlines flight en route to Kathmandu was hijacked and diverted to Kandahar. Azhar's elder brother, Ibrahim Azhar, was among the hijackers, and his brother-in-law Yusuf Azhar, and younger brother Abdul Rauf Asghar (also known as Abdul Rauf Azhar), planned the hijacking.

Azhar returned to Pakistan after his release, where he was welcomed as a hero. He even wrote in one of his columns that the IC-814 hijack had avenged Pakistan's defeat in the 1971 Indo-Pakistan war. On 31 January 2000, he was allowed to address a gathering of around 10,000 people in Karachi. Immediately after this event, with the support of the ISI, the new golden boy of local jihad launched a new group, vowing to destroy India and liberate Kashmir.

That group that was launched was the Jaish-e-Mohammed. It was established on 4 February 2000, at a congregation at Masjid Falal in Karachi. Azhar received widespread support from members of his former group Harkat-ul-Ansar, three-quarters of cadres of which were believed to have joined him in Jaish. The JeM was also acknowledged and endorsed by three religious school chiefs, Maulana Mufti Rashid Ahmed of the Dar-ul Ifta-e-wal-Irshad, Maulana Sher Ali of the Sheikh-ul-Hadith Dar-ul Haqqania, and Mufti Nizamuddin Shamzai of the Majis-e-Tawan-e-Islami. Interestingly enough, Ayesha Siddiqa, the famous Pakistani author and military expert, claims in an article: 'I have seen death certificates for martyrdom issued by the JeM in 1999, indicating that the organization existed in some premature form even before 2000.'

In the same article, Siddiqa says:

> Azhar is deeply plugged into the Pakistan military's intelligence setup, or at least those parts of it with which he shares an

appreciation of the need for the Islamic world to have a strong center to provide protection to Muslims all over the world. Azhar is for the Deobandi jihadis what Lt. General Hameed Gul (former head of Pakistan's Inter-Services Intelligence or ISI who was part of the Afghan jihad of the 1980s) was for the ISI–an inspirational figure who is well connected in the jihadi world and resolutely believes in Ghazwa-e-Hind (the battle for a definitive conquest of India) and the ultimate crusade against all non-Muslims. The relationship between certain segments of the intelligence agencies and the JeM is based on a common value system and not merely a tactical need for each other.

The same General Gul, in several conversations we had at his residence, confirmed his closeness to Azhar and his ideology, and how he shared values and ideals with certain segments of the jihadi world. He often harked back to the Pakistani army's years of deep involvement in the Afghan jihad during the 1980s, a period when the Inter-Services Intelligence (ISI), under his leadership and that of others, cultivated close ties with various militant groups. These relationships, forged in the crucible of the anti-Soviet war, did not end with the Soviet withdrawal in 1989. Rather, they evolved into a long-term strategic asset for Pakistan's regional objectives, particularly concerning Kashmir and Afghanistan. By the year 2000, when Masood Azhar founded the Jaish-e-Mohammed, the ISI's relationship with jihadist groups had already spanned nearly two decades. Gul, who had served as Director-General of the ISI from 1987 to 1989, was candid about the enduring utility of such alliances. He described these groups as instruments of policy—used to exert pressure on adversaries while maintaining plausible deniability. Side-note: the general, one of the most entertaining fellows I've ever met, also shared with me his intention to write an essay on the identity of values between the French Revolution and Islam, and many other interesting details on events that developed in the country much later, but that is quite another story.

JeM was founded with the help of the ISI, and the group immediately began to build links and coordinate with other crown jewels of the Pakistan's Deep State jihad—Lashkar-e-Toiba just to mention one. The group's main goals were to unite Kashmir with Pakistan, ensure that Pakistan was ruled by Shariah law, and drive Western forces out from Afghanistan. Its primary objective, however, remains to "liberate" Kashmir from Indian control and integrate it into Pakistan. The group aims to achieve this primary goal by engaging with Indian forces, hoping for their eventual withdrawal from the region. Curiously enough, all these groups claiming to fight jihad for the liberation of Kashmir, as well as the majority of politicians in Pakistan, have never bothered to fact-check history, and read the widely available historical documents. I have been asked in Pakistan more than once, and by Oxford/Cambridge-educated fellows, 'Do you think we'll ever get Kashmir back?' And when you politely reply that well, actually documents in hand tell you that Kashmir has never been a part of Pakistan, you get an empty look and a puzzled smile. They just don't know, or pretend not to.

It might be interesting to mention here, the answers that Hamid Gul and Mohammed Hafiz Saeed gave me on Kashmir and jihad. 'Kashmir is vital for Pakistan,' said General Gul, while stating that LeT was not a terrorist group but a Kashmiri freedom fighter group, and could not be harmed in Pakistan because it had not committed any wrong on Pakistani soil. 'Now more than ever. Before it was only a moral or political issue, now is a life or death matter.' And His Holy Terror Hafiz Saeed said, 'The people of Pakistan and the Pakistani government support the war of liberation in Kashmir.' And of course, they supported the newly-formed jihadi group. A group that became very active in India immediately after its formation, mainly in Jammu and Kashmir, but not exclusively. The first act of suicide terrorism in the Valley was conducted by JeM within a few months of its formation. On 19 April 2000, a suicide car bomb exploded outside the Indian Army's 15 Corp headquarters in Badami Bagh, Srinagar. It was the first 'VBIED' attack, in which two soldiers were killed. This attack emboldened the group significantly. On 1 October 2001, the organisation targeted the State Assembly building in Srinagar with a car bomb. The militants entered the building and engaged in a shootout with Indian Security Forces.

A little more than a month later, JeM, in an operation carried out with Lashkar-e-Toiba, went a step further and attacked the Indian Parliament in Delhi. 'On the rare occasion when Azhar was arrested in December 2001,' comments the same Ayesha Siddiqa, who continues:

> He was not treated like an ordinary prisoner. This was soon after the Indian Parliament attack. In March 2002 he was shifted from Mianwali jail to Bahawalpur and even given a monthly stipend of 10,000 rupees. His sympathizers in intelligence protected him again in 2004 from arrest by the Punjab CTD. Thanks to the patronage of intelligence agencies, successive governments were unable to contain the JeM. In the words of the former Punjab Home Minister Rana Sanaullah, 'We can't touch these organizations because these are controlled from somewhere else'.

And since data is important too, here is a non-exhaustive list of the major attacks carried out in India by the group over the past few years:

- **Rajbagh police station attack:** On 20 March 2015, a fidayeen squad of terrorists in army fatigues stormed a police station on the Jammu-Pathankot National Highway, killing five persons, including three security force personnel and two civilians, while ten others were injured. A note written in Urdu was recovered from the encounter site, which indicated the terrorists' affiliation with JeM. Leads verified the role of the Pakistan terror group in the attack.
- **Tangdhar Army camp attack:** In November 2015, three JeM terrorists attacked the army camp leading to a fire in the oil dump and barracks. One JCO and a civilian were killed, while all the three JeM terrorists were eliminated in the ensuing encounter.
- **Pathankot Air Base attack:** On 2 January 2016, the Air Force base in Pathankot, Punjab, was attacked by terrorists linked to the JeM group. Four terrorist were neutralised by the NSG. Arms and ammunition were recovered from the dead terrorists. Investigative and operational inputs established that the attack was planned and executed by JeM, with the help of the ISI.
- **Nagrota attack:** On 29 November 2016, JeM attacked the Army camp of 166 Artillery Unit at Nagrota, resulting in the killing of seven army soldiers. Maulana Masood Azhar, JeM chief, in his column "Maktoob-e-Khadim" *(Al Qalam)* lauded the attack by terrorists and linked the operation with Muhammad Afzal Guru and "jihad".
- **Attack on DPL Pulwama:** On 26 August 2017 (around 03:40 hrs), a group of JeM fidayeen militants managed to enter the District Police Lines (DPL) in Pulwama. In the ensuing gun battle, eight security personnel, including four from the Central Reserve Police Force (CRPF) and four from Jammu & Kashmir Police (JKP), were killed. Three JeM attackers were also neutralised. Recoveries of weapons and large quantities of arms/ammunition were made.

- **Attack on BSF camp:** On 3 October 2017, JeM fidayeen attacked the 182nd battalion of the BSF camp near Srinagar airport and Air Force station in the Humhama area. Three JeM terrorists were killed in the gun-battle. One BSF personnel was martyred in the incident.
- **Attack on CRPF training camp:** On 31 December 2017, JeM terrorists stormed the 185th battalion camp of the CRPF in Lethpora, Pulwama, in the wee hours, at around 2 am. They first hurled grenades, and then opened fire outside the CRPF camp. They attacked the security guard and managed to get inside. Five CRPF personnel were martyred and three JeM terrorists were killed in the gun-battle.
- **Attack on Indian Army Military Station:** JeM attacked an Indian Army camp in Sunjuwan, J&K, on 10 February 2018, in which six soldiers, three terrorists and one civilian were killed. The attack coincided with the death anniversary of Afzal Guru, a convict of the 2001 Parliament attack.
- **VBIED Attack on CRPF Convoy:** On 14 February 2019, a fidayeen attack was carried out against a CRPF convoy on the National Highway near Lethpora, Awantipora, district Pulwama (J&K). An explosive-laden car rammed into the security force convoy, which resulted in the death of forty CRPF personnel.

There was a spurt in JeM attacks, particularly post the Pathankot attack (January 2016) in the Valley. Synergy among different terror outfits was also recorded in the Valley, with increased sharing of resources and coordination on the ground, for executing attacks. Handlers/militant operatives have been successful in luring and motivating a substantial number of Kashmiri youths to join the *tanzeem* locally. Usually, the hard-core stone-pelters and over ground workers (OGWs) are the potential soft targets exploited by militant operatives and handlers. Local leaders and cadres in the Valley are sensitised for recruiting new cadres, and motivated to impart training in coordination with Hizb-ul-Mujahideen's (HM) local modules.

It would be a big mistake, however, to think that JeM was and is a group whose activities are confined to India. JeM is a member of the United Jihad Council, which was formed in 1990, to bring all Kashmir-focused militant groups under a single banner. It is also an element and an important one at that, of the so-called anti-West coalition in the Afghan-Pak region. The group's agenda spreads well beyond Indian borders. The group has more than once called for the destruction of USA and Israel, culprits of violating rights of Muslims, and to wage jihad against Christians in Europe, to get back the "usurped" Masjid Aqsa in Jerusalem. There have been many statements given by senior cadres and by Masood Azhar himself, in support of the liberation of Palestine, and for the creation of a new front 'to assist the Palestinian Mujahideen in Israel/Palestine to liberate Masjid Aqsa from the Jews'. A new training programme would be created for this. JeM had joined the Afghan Taliban in attacks against the Afghan government, and coalition forces in Afghanistan. A significant number of JeM cadres have since March 2019, been shifted from Pakistan to Afghanistan, and relocated in coordination with the Taliban. Again, presented below is a non-exhaustive list of major JeM attacks in Afghanistan:

- **Attack on a guest house in Kabul:** This took place in May 2015. The November 2015 edition of JeM's publication *Banaat-e-Ayesha*, revealed details of JeM operatives who had been "martyred" in the attack, although the operation was officially claimed by the Taliban.
- **Attack on the Indian Consulate:** On 3 January 2016, an attack on the India Consulate at Mazar-e-Sharif in the Balkh province was conducted by the JeM. The attackers (three) had inscribed on a wall with their own blood:

'Afzal Guru ka Intekam—Ek Shaheed, Hazaar Fidayeen.'
Translation: 'Revenge of Afzal Guru, one martyr, thousand fidayeen.'

- **Attack on Indian Consulate:** Six suicide attackers targeted the Indian Consulate in the Afghan city of Jalalabad on 3 March 2016, killing three civilians and injuring 19 more. The powerful explosions blew out the windows of a nearby building, and destroyed eight cars.
- **Attack on diplomatic area:** JeM cadres of Pakhtun origin carried out an attack on the diplomatic area of Kabul on 31 May 2017, in co-ordination with the Taliban/HQN.
- **Ghazni attack:** On the intervening night of 10 and 11 August 2018, the Taliban along with JeM, launched a major night-time assault on the Afghan city of Ghazni, on the key highway between Kabul and Kandahar. A number of JeM militants belonging to Dal, Bagatu and Babutang areas of District Hangu, KPK, were involved in the Ghazni attack. "Mujahideen" from Waziristan and the Punjab also took part in the Ghazni operation. The last rites of slain militants were performed in Peshawar and at other places. JeM also organised a special prayer for the killed terrorists, at Jazu Maidan in Peshawar.

It is worth mentioning that it was JeM, and not the Taliban as is widely believed in Europe, that kidnapped and killed, in January 2002, the US journalist Daniel Pearl. For Pearl's death, Ahmed Omar Sayeed Sheikh, one of JeM's founding members, was found guilty and sentenced to death. Talking of global agenda and jihad waged against the West, JeM was involved in training one of the terrorists who carried out the attack on the London public transport system in July 2005. James Cromitie, one of the four people arrested in New York in May 2009 for plotting to attack the NYC Synagogue, had apparently expressed the desire to join the JeM. But how did he know of a "local", semi-unknown to the western majority, a group like the JeM? The answer would surprise the reader. Besides having a very close-knit network in Afghanistan with the Taliban and the Haqqani Network, JeM also collaborates with a number of global terrorist groups in the region, including the Uzbek, Tajik, Uighurs, Chechen and the Arabs. These fighters are part of the Al Qaida, Islamic Movement of Uzbekistan (IMU), Islamic Jihad Union (IJU), Katibat al Imam al Bukhari (KIB), Al Qaida in the Indian Sub-continent (AQIS), Afghan Taliban, Islamic State Khorasan Province (ISKP), East Turkistan Islamic Movement (ETIM) and other outfits. Jaish-e-Mohammed also has a very close alliance with a number of terrorist groups in the region including Afghan Taliban, the Haqqani Network (HQN), Al Qaida (AQ), Harkat-ul-Jihad-ul-Islam (HuJI), Harkat-ul-Mujahideen (HuM), Sipah-e-Sahaba Pakistan (SSP), Lashkar-e-Jhangvi (LeJ), Lashkar-e-Toiba (LeT) and Hizbul Mujahideen (HM).

Of Old and New Alliances
Al Qaida
Maulana Masood Azhar was associated for a very long time with Osama Bin Laden. He had fought alongside the Al Qaida against the US troops in Somalia, and had participated in the training of Al Qaida supporters in Yemen. His role in Yemen placed him within the inner ideological and strategic circles of transnational jihad. After the formation of the JeM in 2000, Azhar reportedly travelled to Afghanistan to meet Osama Bin Laden (OBL). JeM also shared the training facilities of Al Qaida in Afghanistan. On one occasion when OBL's bodyguards were dispatched to the frontlines to combat the forces of the Northern Alliance, they

were replaced by armed cadres of the JeM, to provide immediate protection. In 1993, Azhar was in contact with leaders of the Al-Itihaad Al-Islamiya, an Al Qaida-aligned Somali group, that had requested money and recruits from Harkat-ul-Mujahideen (HuM). Azhar visited Somalia and also helped bring Yemeni mercenaries to Somalia.

Lashkar-e-Toiba (LeT)/Indian Mujahideen (IM)

Mohammed Ali, also known by his aliases Mohammed Adil and Waleed, was a key Jaish-e-Mohammed (JeM) operative who ran the "Waleed-Nayeem Module" operating along the Indo-Nepal border. His arrest in November 2011 led to a significant counter-terrorism breakthrough, resulting in the capture of over 15 Indian Mujahideen (IM) operatives across Bihar, India. During his interrogation, he confessed the failure of JeM in carrying out suicide attacks in India in 2010, including a planned assassination of Dr Pravin Togadia. His handler in Karachi, Mohammed Nayeem, introduced him to Iqbal Gheelani, a senior Lashkar-e-Toiba (LeT) operative. Gheelani, in turn, connected him with the Bhatkal brothers—Riyaz and Yasin Bhatkal—key figures in the IM network. During his second visit to India, Adil came under the direct command of Yasin Bhatkal (alias Sidibappa), who became his ultimate handler. In June 2011, in a parallel investigation, the Madhya Pradesh police had arrested 22 hardcore SIMI/IM operatives. Among them was Dr Abu Faisal, a key IM leader from Tata Nagar, Mumbai, closely associated with the notorious absconder Abdus Subhan Qureshi. Another arrested operative, Izazuddin (alias Riyaz, alias Abdullah Bhai), revealed that he had been sent to Mecca by Faisal to establish contact with LeT/IM networks. While in Saudi Arabia, this module was introduced to Wali Hasan, a trusted JeM operative and associate of Abdul Rauf Asghar (Masood Azhar's brother). The JeM-IM overlap can possibly be traced back to the years 2003–2004, when several Muslim youth from Bihar in North India, were sent by JeM and ISI-linked operatives for training to Pakistan. This network included figures like Sohrab, who facilitated the travel of young recruits across the border. Concrete evidence of operational coordination between JeM and IM emerged in 2010, with confirmed joint attack planning. In 2009, JeM operatives like Rizwan, received logistical and facilitative support from IM cadres, particularly those based in Bihar.

Sikh Radicals Group
The Pathankot airbase attack in January 2016 revealed Jaish-e-Mohammed's (JeM) growing ties with Sikh militant elements based in Pakistan, particularly involving early-stage plans for unconventional methods such as paraglider-based attacks. According to reports, Jagtar Singh Tara, the arrested chief of the Khalistan Tiger Force (KTF), had attended a meeting in Sialkot around 2010, where the idea of targeting the Pathankot airbase was discussed. Shahid Latif, a senior JeM commander and one of the handlers of the Pathankot attackers, was also present at this meeting. Tara later confirmed that Latif had identified the airbase as a high-value target during their discussions. More recently, reports have surfaced suggesting that Hardeep Singh Nijjar, a Canada-based Khalistani activist killed in 2023, may have had indirect connections to Shahid Latif through shared ideological and operational spaces in Pakistan, particularly in the Sialkot region.

Rohingya Muslims
The involvement of JeM with Rohingya extremist elements has also been observed in various instances. Indian security forces,

in a counter-terrorism operation undertaken in October 2015 in J&K, neutralised Chotta Burmi, a Rohingya-origin JeM cadre, alongside JeM commander Adil Pathan. Chotta Burmi was also reportedly associated with Hafiz Saeed, the leader of Lashkar-e-Toiba (LeT), and had been seen sharing a platform with him in Pakistan. According to intelligence sources, on 16 August 2012, the Bangladesh authorities had arrested an individual of Rohingya origin, Maulana Mohammed Yunus of the Molavir Kata Al Givari Adarsh Dakhil Madrasa, Cox Bazar, Bangladesh. Mohammed Yunus was an associate of the JeM-linked Abdul Hakim module, which had Yunus and Hakim operating at the Cox Bazar end. Their possible mentor and earlier head of this madrasa was Maulana Shabbir Ahmad in Karachi. Investigations have indicated an overlap between Jaish-e-Mohammed (JeM) operational modules active in Bangladesh and Pakistan, particularly in the context of anti-India activities. These groups have also been reportedly involved in a range of criminal enterprises, including the circulation of Fake Indian Currency Notes (FICN) and human trafficking. Bangladeshi authorities have cited such arrests as clear evidence of JeM's attempts to expand its operational base within the volatile Rohingya refugee belt in Cox Bazar and surrounding areas.

Taliban
Jaish-e-Mohammed's (JeM) ideology closely aligns with that of Al Qaida (AQ) and the Afghan Taliban, largely due to their shared Deobandi religious foundation. Masood Azhar has publicly likened JeM's goals to those of Sipah-e-Sahaba, another Deobandi militant group. The link between JeM and the Taliban is strengthened by this common religious and ideological base, as well as by members who were reportedly trained in similar

madrasas at the same times. Soon after Masood's release from Indian custody, the HuM leader travelled to Kandahar to receive blessings from the Taliban, in support of his launching of the JeM. Prior to the US withdrawal from Afghanistan, JeM had stepped up its operations in Afghanistan, and fighting along with the Afghan Taliban, it aided in the reconnaissance of targets, and in attacks against the US/NATO establishments on the directions of the local leadership of Afghan Taliban. Of late, the JeM leadership increased activities in Afghanistan, from Peshawar, KPK. JeM is very active in Peshawar, where several mosques housing Afghan refugees serve as operational hubs. JeM has also established a significant presence in Quetta, Balochistan, which serves as a staging ground for operations in Afghanistan, especially in the Ghazni province via the Chaman border crossing. The group reportedly maintains two bases in Afghanistan: one near Kandahar (between Spin Boldak and Kandahar city), and another in northern Helmand province. JeM utilises routes through Peshawar, Dera Ismail Khan, and Quetta/Balochistan to conduct operations in Afghan provinces such as Kabul, Nangarhar, Khost, Kandahar, Helmand, and Ghazni.

Currently, JeM cadres are active in multiple Afghan provinces, including Nuristan, Kunar, Laghman, Khost, Ghazni, Gilan, Helmand, and Nangarhar.

Hamas
JeM and Hamas share a jihadist worldview, framing their attacks as "resistance" against "infidel" oppressors (India for JeM, Israel for Hamas). JeM's proxy, the People's Anti-Fascist Front (PAFF), and Hamas, both target civilians as "settlers", mirroring TRF's Pahalgam narrative which we shall delve into a little later in the book. Abdul Rauf Asghar announced a "unification" of Hamas with Pakistani

jihadi groups, with JeM gunmen protecting Hamas leaders, signalling a formal alignment. JeM's Bahawalpur complex expanded to 18 acres by 2025, and serves as a recruitment and fundraising hub, potentially supporting joint propaganda with Hamas.

On 5 February 2025, an event was held in Rawalakot, PoK, titled "Kashmir Solidarity and Hamas Operation Al Aqsa Flood Conference". The event was attended by Hamas leaders alongside JeM and Lashkar-e-Toiba (LeT) commanders. Held at Shaheed Sabir Stadium on Pakistan's Kashmir Solidarity Day, the event was a propaganda exercise to link the Kashmir and Palestine conflicts as part of a "pan-Islamic jihad" against India and Israel. Hamas spokesperson Dr Khalid Qaddoumi, Hamas's representative in Iran, was a key attendee, marking Hamas's first confirmed visit to PoK. Other Hamas figures included Dr Naji Zaheer, Mufti Azam, and Bilal Alsallat. JeM attendees included Talha Saif, Asghar Khan Kashmiri, and Masood Ilyas, with LeT and Hizbul Mujahideen leaders also present. JeM gunmen provided security, signalling formal coordination.

The conference featured inflammatory rhetoric, with JeM leaders naming Indian PM Narendra Modi and Home Minister Amit Shah as targets, aligning Kashmir's insurgency with Hamas's "Operation Al Aqsa Flood" (its 7 October 2023, attack on Israel).

Another significant meeting took place in late April 2025, at the heavily guarded headquarters of Jaish-e-Mohammed (JeM) in Bahawalpur, Punjab, Pakistan, where a delegation from Hamas was hosted. This event occurred days before the 22 April 2025 Pahalgam terror attack in Jammu and Kashmir, claimed by The Resistance Front (TRF). The meeting occurred at the Jamia Masjid Subhan Allah complex and took place in late April 2025, with reports emerging around 19–20 April. Intelligence reports confirm Hamas's commanders were present, and welcomed with ceremonial honours, including horses and Hamas flags. But the names of the leaders from both sides were not immediately disclosed. It was most likely that Talha Saif or Rauf Asghar were present, given their frequent presence at Bahawalpur events. According to unverified claims, Pakistani military officials and PoK's Prime Minister attended, suggesting high-level ISI involvement. The meeting was most likely focused on aligning anti-India and anti-Israel narratives, building on the 5 February 2025, narrative.

Indian intelligence suspects the meeting involved sharing Hamas's 7 October 2023 attack tactics, potentially inspiring TRF's Pahalgam attack. What's interesting is that the event was heavily guarded, with JeM's Bahawalpur HQ under strict ISI oversight, making the Hamas visit impossible without ISI logistical and bureaucratic support.

The meeting indicates growing coordination, with JeM hosting Hamas at its ISI-monitored HQ, suggesting shared logistics and propaganda strategies. JeM's protection of Hamas leaders in Rawalakot and their ceremonial welcome in Bahawalpur, signal formal ties as well. The ISI's facilitation of the meetings aligns with Pakistan's post-Article 370 strategy to globalise Kashmir via Palestine parallels, risking international backlash but amplifying jihadist narratives.

A TERROR ENTERPRISE

He is dead.
No, he is alive but very unwell.
He spoke to ministers and generals in Pakistan informing them of his health condition and whereabouts.

In the past three to four years, everything has been said about Masood Azhar and the Jaish-e-Mohammed, so has the opposite of everything. This story is one Mario Puzo would have loved to write if only he had known of Pakistan and its terror organisations. Taking a closer look, Jaish-e-Mohammed is in fact structured and run exactly like an old mafia organisation of the fifties in America or in the south of Italy, and it adopts the same strategies. The "Cupola", the power structure inside the organisation, is in fact mainly based on blood links—the blood running through the veins of members of the family and the blood they shed together, to enhance their power. Because, at the end of the day, everything is about power, and above all, about keeping the power within the family.

In this story, Masood Azhar could well play the role of Don Vito Corleone, the Founder, Father and Godfather of the organisation. Part of the story is more or less known to the public at large. Masood Azhar was born on 10 July 1968 (source: UN Security Council) and grew up in Bahawalpur. His father was a Deobandi cleric. After his graduation from the Jamia Ulum Islamic madrasa, Azhar grew to become a prominent jihadist leader, and a wanted extremist in India. As mentioned before, Azhar was arrested in 1994 in Anantnag, while visiting J&K during a visit to coordinate the activities of the terror group, Harkat-ul-Jihad-al-Islami. HuA tried its best to get Masood released from Indian custody, but failed. This is where the family begins to rear its head. He was released along with two other terrorists in exchange for hostages, only after an Indian Airlines flight en route to Kathmandu was hijacked and diverted to Kandahar. This was in 1999.

Azhar's elder brother Ibrahim Azhar was among the hijackers, and his brother-in-law Yusuf Azhar and younger brother Abdul Rauf Asghar planned the hijacking. Azhar was welcomed in Pakistan and allowed to address a gathering of around 10.000 people in Karachi. Immediately after, with the support of the ISI, they launched a new group vowing to destroy India and liberate Kashmir. The group was the Jaish-e-Mohammed. A year after its foundation, it carried out an attack on the Indian Parliament. Since then, it has been thriving, and has expanded its activities and functions. What is less known in this story, is that the JeM works as a family-run enterprise in perfect mafia style. And that, in perfect mafia style, the legal activities of the group function independently, and cover up the illegal ones—straight from the pages of Mario Puzo's book. The terror group owns large tracts of properties in Pakistan, and in Pakistan-administered Kashmir, including madrasas, training centres and real estate outfits, from where its charity organisation, the Al Rahmat Trust, runs its offices

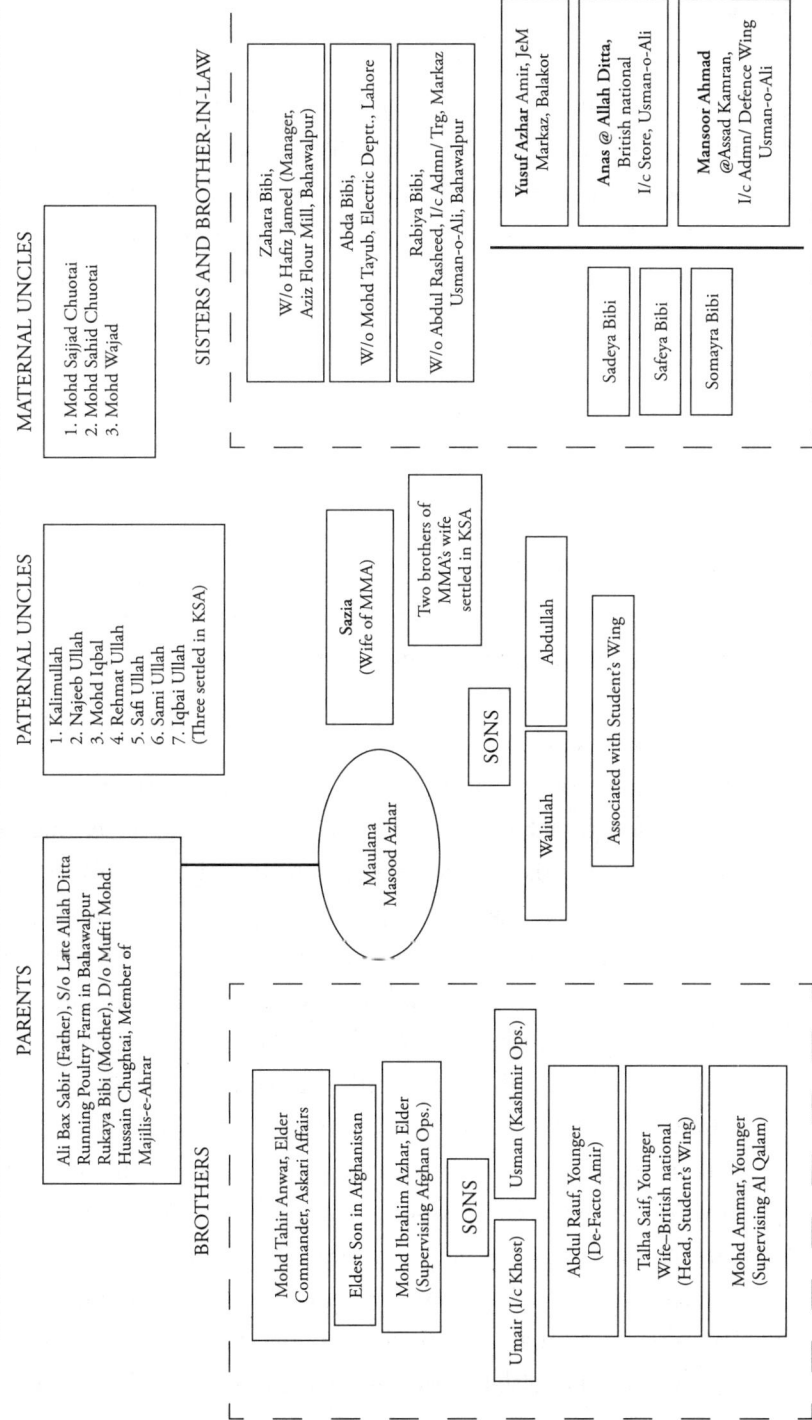

across the country. It is important to note that the distance between charities and terrorism-financing in Pakistan, is particularly blurry.

Pakistan has been in fact, for years, on the "grey list" of the Financial Action Task Force (FATF), and the ambiguity of the charity oversight is the key problem behind this. While several local NGOs engage in admirable work, others are different. In fact, multiple charities have been directly linked to terrorist groups over the past decade. For example, this link was a direct one in the case of Hafiz Saeed, who was one of the founders of a prominent terrorist group (Lashkar-e-Toiba), and at the same time, head of charitable foundations in Pakistan. Similarly, the terrorist group Jihad bi al-Saif, has been linked to the charity Tablighi Jamaat. Other groups have actively used charities to promote their fundraising, and JeM is one of the most active amongst them.

Al Rahmat Trust

Al Rahmat Trust (also spelled Al-Rehmat Trust) is an organisation that has been identified by multiple governments and counterterrorism agencies as a front for Jaish-e-Mohammed (JeM). While it ostensibly operates as a charitable or humanitarian entity, Al Rahmat Trust is accused of supporting JeM's terrorist activities, including fundraising, recruitment, and logistical support. The trust was launched by Masood Azhar in 2002, immediately after the Jaish-e-Mohammed was (in theory) proscribed in 2002. It has been flourishing since then. According to their website, the organisation has been set up in order to provide: 'Struggle to Predominance of Deen, Social Services, Construction of Mosques, Purification of Soul, Support of Shuhada and Ghazian's homes, Struggle for Islamic Captives, Revivalist of Sunnah, Curriculum of basic religious education, Preaching of Islam, Islamic Madaris, Islamic Media'. It is important to note that the Al Rahmat Trust has been instrumental in the recruitment and sponsorship of militants fighting in Afghanistan, Pakistan and Indian administered Kashmir. The JeM/ART is one of the influential Pakistan-based terror organisations that have inspired militancy in Muslim youth, especially among the British and American diaspora. In the past, JeM has had active ties to a number of high-profile terrorist suspects, including Rashid Rauf (the Trans-Atlantic airline bomb plot), Shaykh Ahmad Omar (the Daniel Pearl case), James Cromitie (the Bronx synagogue plot) and two of the July 2005 London suicide bombers, Shehzad Tanweer and Siddique Khan. The trust was in fact sanctioned by the US Treasury Department on 4 November 2010 for being a front organisation for JeM:

> JEM is a Pakistan-based terrorist group designated in October 2001 by the United States pursuant to E.O. 13224 and by the UN 1267 Committee, and also designated as a Foreign Terrorist Organization (FTO) by the State Department in 2001. After it was banned in Pakistan in 2002, JEM began using al Rehmat Trust as a front for its operations. Al Rehmat Trust has provided support for militant activities in Afghanistan and Pakistan, including financial and logistical support to foreign fighters operating in both countries. In early 2009, several prominent members of al Rahmat Trust were recruiting students for terrorist activities in Afghanistan. Al Rahmat Trust has also been involved in fundraising for JEM, including for militant training and indoctrination at its mosques and madrasas. As of early 2009, al Rehmat Trust had initiated a donation program in Pakistan to help support families of militants who had been arrested or killed. And in early 2007, al Rehmat Trust was raising funds on behalf of Khudam-ul Islam, an alias for JEM. Al Rehmat Trust has also provided financial support and

other services to the Taliban, including financial support to wounded Taliban fighters from Afghanistan.

Despite this, ART remained active, continuing their jihadi activities from Bait Al Rahmat, with its address on 3, Railway Link Road, Bahawalpur, Pakistan. Al Rahmat Trust has four regional centres based in Muzaffarabad (PoK), Peshawar, Quetta and Hyderabad (Pakistan). It is further divided into divisional offices of Gujranwala, Bahawalpur, Rawalpindi, Multan, Lahore, Northern Punjab, Karachi and Peshawar Division. Officially, it claims that its objective is to obey Islam, to serve Islam, to spread Islamic education and to help others. Unofficially, as it does in the case of NGOs linked to Lashkar-e-Toiba and Mohammed Hafiz Saeed, the fund collection for the organisation is mainly done for waging "jihad", and to assist families of those who are killed while "waging jihad". In more simple terms, this refers to the act of carrying out terror acts and assisting families of dead terrorists. In the past, the organisation has been providing services to the Taliban as well.

On 10 May 2019, the Pakistan government banned ART in order to demonstrate their compliance with the FATF recommendations. Authorities also released notices asking the general public to refrain from donating to these terror outfits. Yet, the groups were permitted to collect donations under pseudonyms or under the cover of religion throughout the Ramadan period of May–June 2019. JeM also continued their fund collection in Pakistan without issuing receipts to donors, thereby leaving no trails that funding was continuing to these banned groups. ART, in fact, disguised as Al-Masjid, Shohda-e-Asiran, Shoda-e-Umoor and Usman Welfare Trust, continues to carry on funding activities for JeM. The Usman Welfare Trust carries out fund collection in the name of social and welfare work, like blood donation camps in Pakistan. In 2021, this trust has sent food items, clothing and medicine, etc. amounting to PKR 10-15 lakh in the name of assistance to Palestine.

Markazi Bait-ul-Maal, the Central Treasury of Al Rahmat Trust, is responsible for the collection of donations. It often organises "Dauras", gatherings at various centres to mobilise people, and to urge them to donate. ART seeks donations from the public for jihad also, as well as for taking care of families of the killed/arrested militants. It also issues banners urging Muslims to donate the "Ushr" (benefit from the wheat crop), for religious activities at madrasas, and for financial assistance to "deserving" Muslims. It organises campaigns for the collection of "Jehad Fund" for terrorists, and for the funding of their expenses including clothing, arms and ammunitions. Then there is the "Nusrat Fund". The amount collected under Nusrat Fund is under the discretion of Maulana Masood Azhar for further allotment. ART also conducts fund collections titled "Infaq Fi Sabilillah Muhim" (spend in the way of Allah), urging Pakistani Muslims to spend generously in the path of Allah. They are also urged to contribute for fulfilling the requirements of the needy, and for promoting welfare. Apart from donations, the collection of hides of animals sacrificed on the eve of Eid-ul-Azha, also provides large sums of money to JeM.

In 2018, the JeM generated PKR 700 million (approx. Euro 3.9 million), just by selling these animal hides. During Ramadan, appeals are made to Muslims to spend generously in the name of Allah, and to donate for the cause of jihad in Kashmir, as well as to support the jihad in Afghanistan against US/NATO forces. ART's advertisements and writings on different issues like jihad in Kashmir and Afghanistan, regularly appear in JeM's *Al Qalam* newspaper, edited by one of Masood Azhar's younger brothers, and on their web/Facebook pages. The scale of the collection through donations can be seen from the fact that in 2018 alone, the JeM is reported to have collected PKR 600 million (approx. Euro 3.3 million) just from donations.

Back to the Cupola at Home and Abroad
Going back to the Cupola, here is the list of the JeM top leadership:
- Maulana Masood Azhar (MMA), Sarparast-e-Aala/Central Ameer
- Mufti Abdul Rauf Asghar (brother of MMA), de-facto Amir (Head) of JeM/Operational Head
- Talha Saif (brother of MMA), Chief Editor/Publication Wing/Head of Al Mrabitoon (Student Wing of JeM)
- Mohammad Ammar (brother of MMA), supervising *Al Qalam* weekly publication
- Ibrahim Azhar (brother of MMA), supervising Afghanistan operations
- Maulana Yousuf Azhar (brother-in-law of MMA), Amir of JeM's Balakot Markaz, Mansehra
- Abdul Rasheed (brother-in-law of MMA), in-charge of Administration and Training, Markaz Usman-o-Ali, Bahawalpur
- Mohammad Annas (brother-in-law of MMA), in-charge of store at Markaz Usman-o-Ali, Bahawalpur
- Qari Zarrar, Head of Operational/Launching Wing for the Jammu region
- Mufti Asghar Khan Kashmiri, Head of Operations (PoK)/Launching Wing for the Kashmir region
- Maulana Ilyas Qasmi, Head of Dawaati (Invitation and Reformation) Wing

- Maulana Qamar Zaman Siddiqui, Amir, Preaching Wing
- Maulana Mujahid Abbas, Amir Dawaat-o-Islah (Education and Training) Wing

Organisational Structure of JeM

In short, Masood Azhar's brothers and brothers-in-law have full control over the functioning and financing of the group. Abdul Rauf Asghar, Azhar's younger brother, is currently functioning as the de facto Amir of the JeM, possibly due to Masood's ill health. Meanwhile, the two older brothers Ibrahim Azhar and Mohammad Tahir Anwar, are the supervisors of the Afghan operations and the Commander of the JeM's armed cadres, respectively. The other two younger brothers are also important functionaries in the group, with Talha Saif in charge of the student wing, and Mohammad Ammar supervising the weekly publication of the Jaish, Al Qalam. At least four of the six brothers-in-law of Masood are associated with the JeM. Three of them, Mohammad Anas, Mansoor Ahmed and Abdul Rasheed, are involved in various affairs of running the JeM Markaz Usman-o-Ali in Bahawalpur. The fourth, Yusuf Azhar, was in charge of the training camp in Balakot.

In recent years, even the second generation of Masood's family has joined the rank and file of the JeM, in its administrative and operational hierarchy. Azhar's two sons, Abdullah and Waliullah, are involved in operations in Afghanistan and jihadi training respectively. At least three of his nephews have been killed by Indian security forces in J&K over the last few years, where they were heading the JeM's Kashmir operations. The family has also established links abroad. Apart from collections within Pakistan, in fact, a large chunk of ART's funding is received from overseas, especially Saudi Arabia, UAE, Kuwait and Qatar. These funds

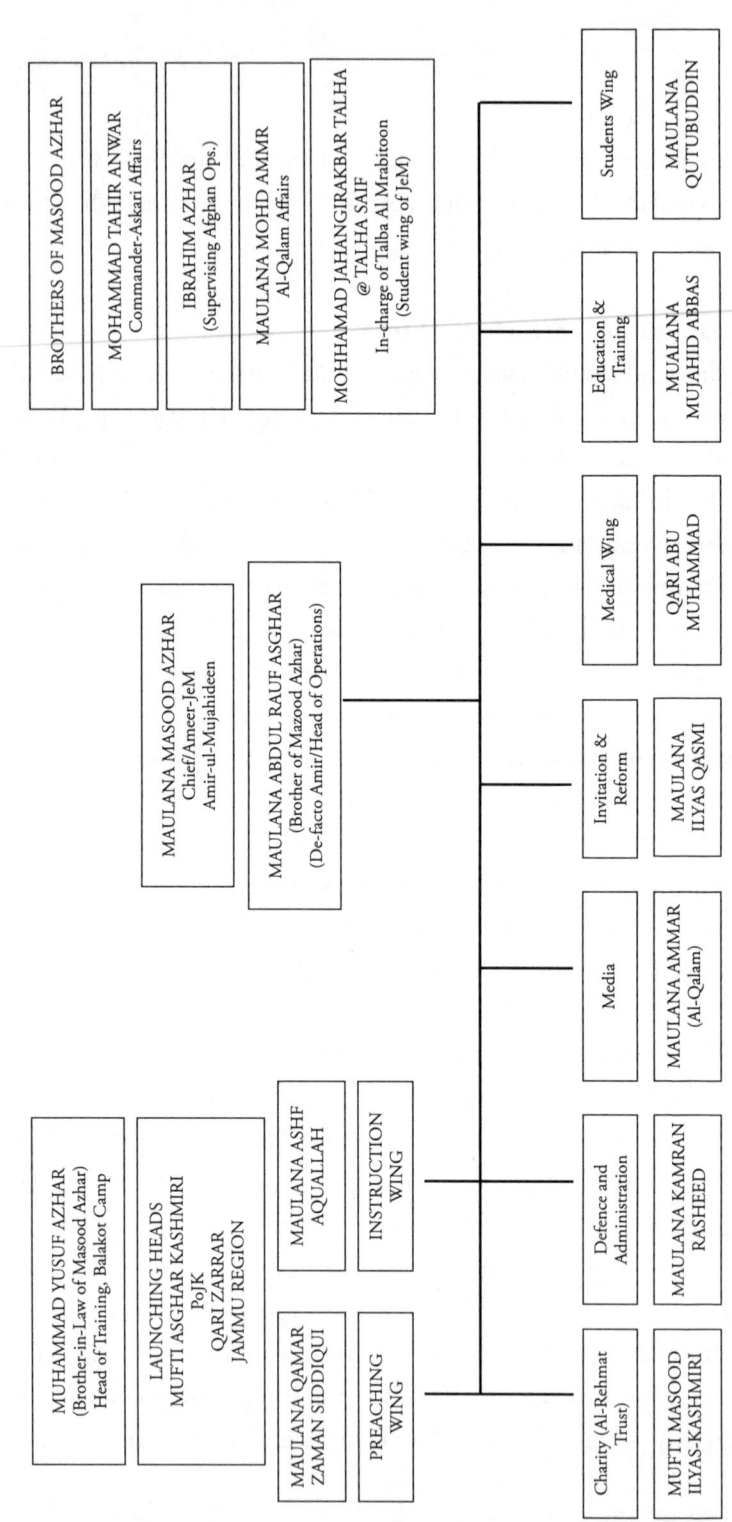

are collected in the name of "Zakat" or for charity work, and the donors are often Pakistani diaspora living in these countries.

Masood's younger brother Talha is married to a British national, and so is his sister Safeya Bibi. Safeya's husband Mohammed Anas handles the stores at the JeM Markaz in Bahawalpur. The family's connections in the UK were built during Masood Azhar's fundraising and recruitment visit to that country in 1993. During that visit, he spoke to large gatherings at mosques and Islamic institutions like the Madina Masjid in Blackburn, and Faizan e Madina mosque in Burnley. According to a BBC report:

> Such was Azhar's popularity in those northern towns that wherever he went, pied-piper like, he accumulated more scholars as part of his entourage. The most surprising engagement of the tour was the speech Azhar gave at what is arguably Britain's most important Islamic institution–a boarding school and seminary in Lancashire known as Darul Uloom Bury. It is also home to Britain's most important Islamic scholar, Sheikh Yusuf Motala.

Azhar's speeches and invocations to taking up jihad as "killing for the sake of Allah", may have inspired and brought many youth into his cause. One of the first recruits to Azhar's new militant group was Mohammed Bilal from Birmingham. Bilal blew himself up outside an army barracks in Srinagar, killing six soldiers and three students in December 2000. But there was another serious consequence of the Masood Azhar connection—the training camp facilities and logistical support he provided to British Muslims willing to carry out attacks in the UK. Several UK-based plots including 7/7, 21/7 and the attempt in 2006 to smuggle liquid bomb-making substances on to transatlantic airlines, are now thought to have been directed by Rashid Rauf, a man from Birmingham, who married into Masood Azhar's family in Pakistan. Rauf's father, Abdul Rauf, helped establish Crescent Relief, an Ilford-based charity that raised over £100,000 for Kashmir earthquake relief in 2005. The Charity Commission investigated claims that these funds may have been diverted to extremist groups, including JeM or its affiliates. While no evidence directly ties Al Rahmat Trust to Birmingham or Rauf, his JeM affiliation and Bahawalpur base (where Al Rahmat operates) suggest he could have interacted with such fronts. The UK's Muslim community, including Birmingham's, may have been targeted for donations despite the fact that in 2014, FATF clearly wrote in its *Risk of Terrorist Abuse in Non-Profit Organisations*:

> On 4 November 2010, al Rehmat Trust, an NPO operating in Pakistan, was designated pursuant to U.S. Executive Order (E.O.) 13224 for being controlled by, acting on behalf of, and providing financial support to designated terrorist organizations, including Al Qaeda and affiliated organizations. Al Rehmat Trust was found to be serving as a front to facilitate efforts and fundraising for a UN designated terrorist organization, Jaish-e Mohammed (JEM). After it was banned in Pakistan in 2002, JEM, a UN 1267 designated Pakistan-based terrorist group, began using Al Rehmat Trust as a front for its operations. Al Rehmat Trust has provided support for militant activities in Afghanistan and Pakistan, including financial and logistical support to foreign fighters operating in both countries. In early 2009, several prominent members of al Rehmat Trust were recruiting students for terrorist activities in Afghanistan. Al Rehmat Trust has also been involved in fundraising for JEM, including for militant

training and indoctrination at its mosques and madrasas. As of early 2009, al Rehmat Trust had initiated a donation program in Pakistan to help support families of militants who had been arrested or killed. In addition, in early 2007, al Rehmat Trust was raising funds on behalf of Khudam-ul Islam, an alias for JEM. Al Rehmat Trust has also provided financial support and other services to the Taliban, including financial support to wounded Taliban fighters from Afghanistan.

Meanwhile, some members of the great JeM family, including brothers of Masood's wife Shazia, and a few of his paternal uncles, are settled in Saudi Arabia. The Al Rahmat Trust is the principal source of income for JeM, and continues to operate despite being sanctioned by several countries. Martin S Navias in *Finance and Security: Global Vulnerabilities, Threats and Responses*, writes:

> ...the charity or NGO uses its facilities or programs to support recruitment of personnel for terrorist organizations. Charities can also supply funds to support the families of terrorists–a very attractive recruitment incentive–or employ their facilities to train and recruit terrorists as well as hosting speakers supporting terrorist organizations. FATF refers to an example of the Pakistani-based al-Rehmat Trust which provided financial support to designated terrorist organizations including Al-Qaeda.

Given the links abroad, it is not a surprise that the terror enterprise has a worldwide funding network. Money comes from UK, Saudi Arabia and European countries. Recently, France has frozen the bank assets of the organisation. Pakistan, of course, did not, and anyway, it would have been useless. Anticipating a possible seizure of assets by the Pakistani government, the

JeM withdrew funds from its bank accounts and invested it in legal businesses, such as commodity trading, real estate, and production of consumer goods. The Jaish-e-Mohammed family, even though it lacks a Michael Corleone, did long ago what any other mafia family would—networking and penetrating State and Deep State, and at a given point, financing its own illegal activities with profits of perfectly legal activities and vice versa.

So, in the past few years, despite all Pakistan's promises to come down on terrorist groups and dismantle their financial hubs, JeM has been more active than ever. It launched, for example, a "Burma Campaign" for the collection of funds for Rohingya Muslims. Maulana Masood Azhar, in his column "Maktoob-e-Khadim" in 2017, urged people to donate for Rohingya Muslims at the JeM headquarters or district centres. It had also released contact numbers of their centres at Markaz Usman-o-Ali, Balochistan, Karachi (East), Karachi (West), Sindh (Interior), KPK, POK, Punjab (North), Punjab (South) and Hazara, with an appeal to donate for Rohingya Muslims. And, unlike the figures officially shown for charities abroad, the numbers of the "donations" and financial activities in Pakistan are quite astonishing.

The JeM annual budget, the budget of the family enterprise, is difficult to understand or show in full, due to obvious reasons. In 2018 in particular, the amount generated annually by selling animal hides was PKR 70 crores. According to sources, the amount received in the form of donations was more or less PKR 60 crores, and payments from ISI exclusively for jihadi operations, was PKR 1 crore per month (PKR 12 crores annually). Collections from land, cattle, wheat, rice, grains, etc. are taken separately. The average monthly expenditure of JeM from all over Pakistan between January and June 2018 was around PKR 5–6 crores. This budget did not include expenditure on constructions of mosques, markaz or madrasas. More recently, in 2021, JeM had collected "Nafil Qurbani" of 5,000 animals (fund collection for 5,000 sacrificial animals) during the Eid-ul-Adha. They, in fact, succeeded in collecting an amount exceeding PKR 30 crores, as against the targeted amount of PKR 27 crores as "Ushr" collection during the month of Ramadan 2021. In fact, they have stated that the fund collection had exceeded their own expectations, and that they had exceeded the targeted "Qurbani" fund collection for the year.

In the past few years, JeM intensified its fund collection drive. It collected funds through various campaigns like "Qurbani Muhim", "Infaq Muhim" and "Masajid Muhim". "Qarbani Muhim" involved donations of amounts ranging from PKR 500 to PKR 1,000 by each cadre in place of animal hides, as the prices of hides had come down in the market during Eid-ul-Zuha, due to restrictions imposed on their collection, due to FATF/APG pressure. While "Infaq Muhim" was launched to collect a specified targeted amount, "Masjid Muhim" (fund collection for construction of new mosques) was intensified after Eid-ul-Zuha 2021. Under this campaign, 17 new mosques are to be constructed in Pakistan by JeM. JeM has already acquired a new masjid named Masjid Hamza at Sialkot, and they are planning another at Badiana near Daska in Sialkot on the Pasrur Road. JeM's fund collection campaigns also include "Jehad Fund" (for general terrorism), "Infaq fi Sabil Allah Muhim Fund" (to collect funds for jihad in Kashmir), and "Nusrat Fund" (donation of Pakistani currency of Rs 50).

In recent years, according to observers, '…there has been a significant increase in enrolment in basic induction courses, religious programs and jihadi training courses organised by JeM at their centres in Pakistan.' Going through the lists of expenditures, the calls for donations of the enterprise is almost hilarious. They circulate pamphlets, through Al Rahmat, asking for donations to provide winter equipment for poor mujahideen fighting against enemies. The full kit of the perfect terrorist costs PKR 10,000, including PKR 2,500 (for boot/shoes), PKR 2,000 (warm bedding), PKR 1,200 (blanket), PKR 1,800 (clothing), PKR 1,600 (jacket), PKR 500 (socks and caps) and PKR 400 (inner wear).

There is a very interesting list that allows the donor to provide assistance to a mujahideen fighting in Afghanistan or J&K, a kind of "adopt a mujahideen" programme. You will be able to set up and equip any guy, turning him from a poor useless, illiterate fellow, into a war machine. From the list provided, you'll find out that you have to spend PKR 5,00,000 to convert a poor chap into a perfect holy warrior, providing both spiritual and physical training, while a Kalashnikov costs much less—PKR 1,35,000 only! It is not clear whether they are giving wholesale or retail market prices, but that list is comprehensive.

Then, if you are really motivated, you can add PKR 90,000 to buy bullets or PKR 10,000 for a full mujahideen outfit. You can also cover the expenses for a lawyer, in case your pet mujahideen is arrested, and that amounts to PKR 80,000. Tom Hagen might not been there as "Consigliere" for the Jaish, but the Pakistani version of the Corleone family takes good care of its men, like any other mafia family does of its members. It has allocated a budget of PKR 3.5 crores for 2,300 family members of terrorists. Further, an amount of PKR 5 crores has been allocated for meeting expenditures including legal fees towards the release of 1,400 cadres. Families of martyrs or Gazis (returned fighters) get PKR 1,20,000.

There are also other creative ways to collect money. For

example, Qari Zarrar, a JeM commander, liaises with Pak ISI for arms and ammunition. He is also involved in the selling of high-end cars purchased from Afghanistan. Some of these vehicles are utilised for JeM's work, while the remaining are sold in the grey market to finance Jaish's activities. And, since Al Rahmat's web page states that no donation is too small, JeM has issued "Receipt Books" of PKR 50 denomination for its cadres who were asked to collect funds from the general public as part of this campaign. JeM also asked its cadres to renew their efforts to increase the sale of its publication, *Risala*, among the masses, to propagate JeM's ideology, thereby also increasing funding. Trainees undergoing the "Daura-e-Tarbiya" course, have also been encouraged to sell the JeM magazine *Madina-Madina*, costing PKR 10 per copy, to at least ten of their friends and relatives.

Earlier, in 2019, JeM had conducted the "Daura-e-Tafseer" at seventy-three places in various districts of Pakistan. In Italy, Nicola Limodio conducted a study for Bocconi University. Nicola Limodio's study, "Terrorism Financing, Recruitment, and Attacks", was published in *Econometrica* in July 2022. The paper examines how variations in local financing, influenced by a Sharia-compliant institution in Pakistan, affect terrorist activities. The research utilises data from jihadist-friendly online forums operating on the dark web. A random subset of messages from these forums was also evaluated by two judges, who determined whether the content exhibited recruitment intent. At a point, Limodio states:

> A Sharia-compliant institution in Pakistan induces exogenous variation in the funding of terrorist groups through their religious affiliation. I isolate the supply of terrorist attacks by following multiple terrorist groups with different affiliations operating in various cities. Higher terrorism financing, in a

given location and period, generates more attacks in the same location and period. This effect increases in recruitment, measured through dark-web data, inputs by two judges and machine-learning. This evidence is consistent with terrorist organizations facing financial frictions to their internal capital market.

It is that simple—more money, more attacks.

OF TERROR AND TRAINING

The Balakot camp is again fully operative in both sections, the religious and the military one. In the past months, 100–150 boys in the age group between 9 and 18 years have started their training and their indoctrination in religion and theology. And at least 35 cadres of JeM have started their military training there, under the supervision of senior JeM functionaries like the Operational Commander Abdul Rauf Ashgar. Launching Commander Qari Zarrar and Ibrahim Azhar have also visited the Balakot camp to supervise the training.

According to my local sources, a year after the Indian operation, the Balakot camp was once again fully operative. The training activities that were halted after the Indian Air Force airstrike on 26 February 2019, had resumed in mid-April 2019. Initially, only religious courses started inside the markaz. The "Askari" or military training resumed in August 2019. Though Pakistan denied the existence of a training camp at Balakot, and also denied that the strikes had destroyed the camp leading to casualties, on numerous occasions, there has been an indirect acceptance of the strikes by former Pakistan Prime Minister Imran Khan.

According to locals:
In the last week of October, Pakistani authorities, fearing an impending attack on the facility by India, directed JeM functionaries to vacate the camp of trained cadres. However, the theological course continued at the camp in the presence of senior functionaries. Military training resumed again in the second week of January 2020, and JeM cadres were again undergoing training there.

The same locals maintain that the Balakot camp continues to be under the supervision of Maulana Yousuf Azhar, W of the JeM Chief Masood Azhar. The elder brother of Masood Azhar, Ibrahim Azhar, is believed to be in charge of JeM's operations in Kashmir. He has visited Pakistan-controlled Kashmir a number of times in the past few years. According to sources, JeM has been directed by its Pakistani Army and intelligence handlers to plan targeted attacks in Kashmir. For this purpose, the group has also started recruiting fidayeen cadres. Mufti Abdul Rauf Asghar, brother of Masood Azhar, has been placed in charge of the recruitments. The rest of the Azhar family, which is practically a mafia/terror enterprise, is still very active, despite all the talks by the Pakistani government about acting against terrorist organisations. Nothing has changed it seems, least of all the support of the State to jihadi groups. Rauf Asghar, despite at a point being placed officially under protective custody, has been seen holding multiple meetings with ISI operatives. Maulana Ammar and Talha Saif, both younger brothers of Masood Azhar, were seen by locals on 16 January 2020 in Peshawar, attending the release of a book by Masood Azhar, titled *Saifullah-e-Nishbat*. Islamabad has been claiming that the leader of Jaish-e-Mohammad has disappeared with his family. Masood Azhar meanwhile, has been seen by multiple witnesses roaming freely all over Pakistan. It seems that the most famous beard of the country has been moving around all this time. Eye witnesses have confirmed seeing Azhar at the Markaz Usman-o-Ali and Markaz Subhan Allah in his hometown in Bahawalpur, between 10–25 November 2020. He has also addressed JeM cadres during this period. The same eyewitnesses also added that Masood Azhar went to Bahawalpur in January 2020, to see his ailing mother, and that he travelled to Rawalpindi in early February, immediately before Pakistan declared him "missing".

As of latest reports, Azhar is believed to be residing in Bahawalpur, Pakistan, under heavy security. He has been provided safe houses in densely populated areas, such as near the Osman-o-Ali Masjid and the National Orthopaedic and General Hospital, to deter potential operations against him. In December 2024, Azhar reportedly delivered an anti-India address at the Markaz Subhan Allah, urging youth to join the fight. And eyewitnesses confirmed Azhar's presence on 8 May 2025 in Bahawalpur, at the funeral rites for family members killed in Indian air strikes. In brief, despite all the smoke that Islamabad is generating to cover up the truth from the international community in general and the FATF in particular, JeM has continued carrying out all its activities in the past few years. After the Balakot strike and after the FATF lifted the ban, religious courses started again at Markaz Usman-o-Ali, Bahawalpur. Similar courses have resumed in other JeM centres, in Karachi first and then in Peshawar, at the Markaz Sanan bin Salma, with the help of Taliban commanders and trainees. Locals believe that most of the trainees will be sent to infiltrate Kashmir.

JeM has also resumed collecting funds for jihad all over the country. The fund collection for the so-called "Nusrat Fund" continues. People believe that JeM has collected at least Pakistani Rs 6 crores from Peshawar and the bordering areas of Afghanistan. According to western police investigations, a portion of the fund has also been received through overseas Pakistanis. The JeM charity wing, Al Rahmat Trust, has been circulating pamphlets seeking donations for the group in a more clandestine fashion, to avoid being noticed by the FATF. People are being encouraged to donate money to fund the purchase of uniforms and other daily requirements of JeM Mujahideen.

Despite the so-called arrest of Mohammed Hafiz Saeed, the LeT/JuD continues to operate freely as well. The group has been collecting funds in the name of Khidmat committees for carrying out jihad in Kashmir. Top leaders of the group also continue to deliver sermons and address large crowds. In order to prevent coming to the adverse notice of the FATF, Hafiz Saeed, Abdur Rehman Makki, Yahya Mujahid and some other senior leaders who were in "protective custody", were told to maintain a low profile and limit their activities. However, as usual, they had full access to all their resources.

A year after the Indian Air Force airstrike, not only was Balakot active again, but the whole structure of JeM and other jihadi groups was alive and kicking. They were ready to be used at the right moment, despite all of Islamabad's claims. Being unsuccessful in conventional wars with India, Pakistan in connivance with the ISI, has for many years been pursuing a low cost proxy war to annex Kashmir by using terrorism as a weapon and fomenting trouble in the Valley. The ISI is instrumental in sponsoring militancy in J&K, facilitating training, funding, indoctrination, logistics, infiltration, providing of arms, communication tools (satellite phones, internet-based mobile communications, GPS, coded matrix sheets, etc), refurbishing/

construction of launching hubs, besides support to the families of killed militants.

To fulfil its objective, it has been funding, training and arming terrorist groups like Jamaat-ud-Dawa (JuD)/Lashkar-e-Toiba (LeT), Jaish-e-Muhammad (JeM), Hizbul Mujahideen (HM) and Al-Badr. The cadres are recruited in the name of waging jihad against the "infidels" for "liberating" Kashmir from India. Charity fronts of terrorist groups like Falah-e-Insaniyat Foundation (FIF) of JuD and Al Rahmat Trust of JeM, raise funds for supporting terrorism in Kashmir and elsewhere, in the garb of welfare activities. Millions of Pakistani rupees are collected in the form of donations such as Zakat and Ushr, and from sacrificial hides sold during Eid. These groups continue to collect funds, organise anti-India events and propagate "jihad", with the tacit support of the official machinery. Terrorist groups and their politico-religious front organisations operate chains of mosques, madrasas and big religious complexes/centres (markaz) across Pakistan, and Pakistan Occupied Jammu and Kashmir (PoJK).

After the Indian air strikes on JeM camps in PoJK/Pakistan, the area was declared out of bounds by Pakistani Security Forces for days. No journalist was permitted to visit the location. But Balakot, as the rest of the world knows and the other part just pretended not to know, was for sure not the only training camp in Pakistan. If you do not want to trust intelligence on the issue, just ask the long, long string of Pakistanis asking for asylum in Italy. Whatever Islamabad says, Pakistan still has training camps running, alive and kicking in PoK. The country has been having them for the last couple of years, despite all the denials they furbish, and the mocking of any kind of evidences given by experts and journalists. It is stated into a sentence by the Tribunal of Perugia (sentence number Nr. 3213\2019 R.G. 30 June 2020) regarding a refugee case. Quoting from it:

> In the appeal it is deduced that Ali (surname not given for obvious reasons), was born and raised in Karachi, Pakistan, where he earned the title of mechanical engineer and worked as a freelancer professional; that he is of Sunni Muslim religion, and in 2015 attended a course in to whom Islamic rules were imparted; in 2017 he went to Kashmir for attend again a course of the aforementioned group; was taken to a center of training to carry out a "training" which consisted of training physical and use of weapons for the purpose of Jihad; finished the course, he returned home; subsequently people of the Islamic group "Lashkar-e-Taiba" asked him to join the group; the applicant invented excuses to reject the invitation; this caused their wrath; when he learned they were organizing his kidnapping decided to leave Pakistan for Italy.

This, in the convoluted language of an Italian Tribunal sentence, is the story of Ali who was granted refugee status by a Tribunal in Perugia. It is a very interesting story for many reasons. According to Ali, in fact, he joined an Islamic integralist centre in Karachi of his own free will. He went to Pakistan-administered Kashmir to join a JeM jihadi training camp of his own free will, and then was back in Karachi. LeT members were trying to force him to join their group—a group which apparently he had already joined the moment he went to a training camp. When he tried to give up jihad, according to his fantastic story, LeT along with ISI planned to kidnap him. Alerted by some whistleblower, he decided to leave for Italy, where he asked for political asylum. A first sentence denied him any kind of asylum or refugee status, because the story was frankly full of holes. But then the guy found a good lawyer, appealed against the sentence and found a "good" judge. Somebody who literally reproduced the Wikipedia page about LeT into his judgement, without further interrogation of the petitioner and without even considering the past cases in Italy.

The most well-known case of Pakistani origin, is that of Hafiz Muhammad Zulkifal, the so-called "spiritual guide" of a Lashkar-e-Toiba cell, who was arrested by the Italian police in 2015. The imam lived with a large family in a small house in the Bergamo area. For the tax office, he had no properties, and his income was not enough to support the number of his siblings. So he has been living on Italian taxpayers' money for almost twenty years, all the while preaching against kafirs and the western way of life, and simultaneously training a jihadi cell. He was getting state subsidies for the house rent, subsidies for the schooling of his children, in addition to the family bonuses for large families. He is not the only one to enjoy these. 'Many Pakistanis who apply for asylum,' says a Pakistani journalist living in exile, 'apply four or five times giving different names each time. They arrive via Turkey or Greece and go directly to a refugee camp, without a passport, and without giving their real name. Families and smugglers advise them to talk as little as they can, and to say they are persecuted by the Taliban or other jihadi groups. Or to say they belong to a persecuted minority.'

'The truth is,' says one of the official cultural mediators at a refugee camp, a Pakistani himself, 'They are all Punjabis and I've never seen, except for a few Ahmadiya, somebody belonging to a persecuted minority.' According to people living in the same refugee camp, they often attack individuals belonging to minorities, and "kafirs" in general. After the asylum has been granted, often on the ground of so-called "humanitarian reasons", they join members of their family or their community. And this is most probably how Italy gets Lashkar-e-Toiba cells.

In 2016, a handful of Pakistani citizens were arrested and repatriated due to links with terrorist organisations. Five years ago, a huge police operation in the north of Italy highlighted an eight million Euro network of money illegally sent by Pakistani citizens to terrorist organisations in Afghanistan and Pakistan. According to reports of the Italian intelligence: 'Pakistani nationals who arrived in Italy with no money on immigrant boats and with no significant economic background, suddenly become entrepreneurs.' According to the same sources, these people, strictly with no criminal records, are approached by members of the community, indoctrinated, then protected by foreign agents and placed into the Islamic community. The same intelligence reports highlighted that the funding, done by Pakistani money senders, were intended, 'Not only for radical Islamist jihadist groups acting against the West, but also for entities supported by ISI, that operated and still operate in India.' Pakistani embassies refuse most often to co-operate with intelligence agencies and police, when asked to identify people.

So Italy remains a privileged hub for jihadis and criminals. This is the reality in many other places in Europe as well. Scratch lightly into any of the major attacks in Europe in the past few years, and you will always find a Pakistani connection. Because the jihadi monster created by Pakistan as the privileged tool of foreign politics, has quite often got out of control despite the intentions of the Deep State. So the training camps after Balakot, followed a now habitual modus operandi, the same that is executed after any major attack with international implications. It happened after Mumbai 2008; it has happened after the Pulwama attack. Camps are quickly closed and dismissed, or temporarily disguised as religious schools for children. As soon as the attention of the international media vanishes, everything goes back to normal.

Training camps which were temporarily shut down in the aftermath of Balakot were later revived. Trainings—both indoctrinal (Daura-e-Tarbiya, Daura-e-Asasiya) and military (Daura-e-Zarar, Daura-e-Fida) have resumed at Markaz Saeedana Bilal, Shawai Nullah, Chelabandi in Muzaffarabad, PoJK, in Balakot, Mansehra District, KPK, and in Markaz Subhan Allah, Bahawalpur, Punjab. Ideological and military training to terrorists are provided by leaders and experienced cadres of militant outfits, as well as ISI and Special Services Group (SSG) officers. Leaders of terrorist groups visit mosques and madrasas to deliver religiously charged sermons to motivate people to provide logistics/financial support, and also join jihad against India, especially in Kashmir.

JeM's student wing, Talba Al-Murabitoon, is the main front for the recruitment of cadres. JeM organises a number of events under banners of "Majlis Warsa-e-Shoda Jammu-Wa-Kashmir" and "Majlis Dawat-Al-Quran". Various conference/ congregation/programmes including "Daura Tafseeryat Al-Quran", "Dars-e-Quran", "Azmat Shohda Conference", "Shukr-e-Azaadi Conference", "Seerat-ul-Nabi Conference", "Qayam-e-Pakistan Conference", "Khutba Jumma" (Friday sermons), and conferences in the names of killed/dead militants, are also organised by JeM in Pakistan and PoJK, to motivate people to join the cadre. The Al Rahmat Trust and its Preaching Wing are also actively involved in motivating people for jihad during their various seminars and conferences. They urge the attendees to join their various courses. The prospective cadres for physical and advanced armed/fidayeen training, are then shortlisted from those who attend these basic courses. JeM routinely publishes advertisements of various courses along with their schedule, in its monthly magazine, and posts it all over social media sites as well.

Even during the pandemic, the only organisations that never stopped and never ceased to be active, were in fact the terrorist ones. We know from video and images, for example, that in February 2021 the glorious Jaish-e-Mohammed, headed in the region by Masood Ilyas, was holding rallies in Pakistan Occupied Kashmir, calling for jihad and challenging the rest of the world to come and see that their struggle would never be over. During the same time, perhaps because of the lack of "official" cultural activities, the brave "social workers" of JeM started the re-publication of *Musalmaan Bache* (Children of Islam), one of the main publications of the group, which had been discontinued in the past most probably during one of the whitewashing efforts by the government, in order to exit the FATF grey list. The group is now bringing out four publications regularly.

Amir Masood Azhar has continued to comfort and support his followers even during pandemic time, airing his messages through the social media linked to the group. Perhaps due to the lack of social activities in Pakistan, the group also provided education for the masses, organising a course (Daura Tafseer Ayat al Jihad) at Jamia Masjid Noor Gaon Sokhta in the Charsadda district of KPK, and two other courses, a Daura-e-Asasiya (basic course) and Daura-e-Khair (course on virtue) at its Markaz Usman-o-Ali in Bahawalpur. All this, of course, while the government of Pakistan was for the umpteenth time trying to convince the world of their good faith in cracking down on terrorist organisations, their activities, bank accounts and fund raising. But guess what, it was a lie once again.

In fact, the JeM had not stopped at all. If anything, the group was intensifying its fund collection drive. Before Ramadan in the same year, a number of posters were circulated on social media calling for donations. In one of these posters uploaded on 10 April 2021, the organisation made an appeal calling for donations to complete the construction of the Jamia Siddique Masjid in Peshawar, a masjid affiliated of course, to Jaish-e-Mohammed. Masood Azhar and his goons were not only asking for money, but were on a big recruiting campaign as well. During the month of May, posters calling for new recruitments were mushrooming all over the country. In Kohan district and in three madrasas in Karachi—Jamia Al Noor, Aka Khel Masjid and Bateha Masjid—these posters proliferated. In the same month of May, JeM was posting on social media announcing the opening of admissions for a course on Hifz & Nazra (memorising and understanding Quran). The course was for free and held at the Madrasa Abdullah bin Masood Jangal Khel, Kohat, KPK. The calls to jihad were not limited to Afghanistan or India. In May, the JeM posted a "Maktoob" calling on Islamic countries to immediately consider jihad to liberate Palestine. These messages conveyed that those Islamic countries unable to dispatch armies against Israel "due to the hypocrisy of international laws", should dispatch mujahideens and razakars (volunteers) to take part in jihad, and that they should issue a fatwa against Jews. Again, on 3 January 2022, JeM held a public rally in Jaloth, near Rawalakot, to claim responsibility for a December 2021 attack in Srinagar and to raise funds. The event was addressed by Muhammad Illyas, JeM's PoK chief, and featured fighters firing shots in the air while shouting pro-jihad slogans.

However, in October 2022, Pakistan was nevertheless removed from the Grey List of the Financial Action Task Force (FATF) due to its "significant improvements in the counter-terrorist financing" framework. And yet, while waiting for the sentence and immediately after the removal from the Grey List, the most widely acknowledged base of the JeM in Bahawalpur was undergoing a major expansion. An investigative report published in December 2024 by the French magazine *Le Spectacle du Monde* states that: "According to satellite photos available on the Planet Labs website, Jaish-e-Mohammed has two centers in the Bahawalpur area: Markaz Subhan Allah and the Usman-o-Ali mosque", and uncovers the massive construction work going on at the markaz since 2022. Satellite imagery analysis indicates that Subhan Allah has doubled in size to over 18 acres, nearly twice its original footprint since its construction in 2011–12. As per the report, satellite imagery and eyewitness accounts reveal that these operations occur in plain sight, with one complex located merely eight kilometres from a Pakistani military base. According to Damien Symon, an analyst working with The Intel Lab, the upgraded compound appears to feature multiple new buildings, a mosque, and livestock stables. The latest satellite image, dated 10 January 2025, provided by space technology firm Maxar Technologies, confirms that construction is still ongoing. According to the same images, security measures have been reinforced, demonstrating an effort to fortify the site. A report published by *India Today's* Open-Source Intelligence (OSINT) team, confirms that a JeM gathering took place at this location, as recently as 16 February 2025. The event, a fundraising part of "Infaq fi Sabilillah" (spending in the way of Allah) campaign, was addressed by Talha al-Saif, brother of Masood Azhar. Azhar himself, after many months of "disappearing", resurfaced on 27 June 2024, attending a wedding ceremony and addressing a gathering.

So all this, while JeM from that very same Pakistan that claims to have acted against terrorists, continues to flourish, recruit, raise funds, contest elections and instigate violence across the globe, in any country except for China (let us not forget treatment of their Uyghuri brothers), the government in Islamabad was playing the game of the three monkeys, even while trying to feed the rest of the world their failed narrative. The truth is, for Pakistan, terrorist groups are their biggest and practically only asset. They are the main leverage used successfully for years to convince the rest of the world of the necessity to finance, cajole and arm Pakistan, so that there would be some sort of dystopian peace in the area. Let's go into details.

Basically, two types of training are provided to militant cadres:

Daura-e-Aam—a basic screening phase where potential terror recruits are identified. It is to filter and identify the more radical and physically fit participants.

Daura-e-Khaas—a second phase of training in field craft, weapons training, navigation, endurance and survival skills. Terrorist groups and their politico-religious front organisations operate chains of mosques, madrasas and big religious complexes/centres (markaz) across Pakistan and PoJK, including Gilgit-Baltistan. As per acceptable figures, there are 18 functional terrorist training camps including 11 in PoJK, which are in the districts of Muzaffarabad (5), Kotli (5), and Bhimber (1); five in the Mansehra district of Khyber Pakhtunkhwa (KPK); and two in Punjab, in the districts Sheikhupura and Bahawalpur. Terrorist cadres are mainly recruited from the Pakistan provinces of Punjab and KPK, besides those from PoJK who are mainly being coerced into joining terrorist groups for "jihad" in Kashmir. Here is a detailed list:

- **Bahawalpur Complex, Punjab:** The camp is spread over approximately eighteen acres of land and has a boundary wall on all sides. According to locals, a number of small- and medium-sized buildings and barracks are there inside the camp, along with a mosque. The complex is located at a distance of approximately 5 kms south-west of Bahawalpur on the northern side of Bahawalpur by-pass on the National

Highway (NH-5). JeM conducts various training programmes at its headquarters at Markaz Usman-o-Ali, and at Markaz Subhan Allah as well, which acts as an extension of Markaz Usman-o-Ali. Markaz Subhan Allah has good infrastructure and facilities, including swimming and archery, which could be utilised by JeM for training as well as to recruit new cadres. According to the same locals, JeM has of late, incorporated swimming and deep diving courses as part of the advance training of its cadres. Often referred to as "New Abbottabad" due to the bin Laden-like proximity with Pakistani military institutions, the site is just 6 kilometres from the Bahawalpur Army Cantonment and 10 kilometres from the Bahawalpur Air Force Station.

- **Shawai Nalla, Muzaffarabad:** This is an office cum transit camp. It is located 400 metres from the Sadr Police Station, Shawai Nalla, Muzaffarabad. It consists of a double-storey building with a capacity to accommodate 100–150 persons.
- **Chelabandi Camp, Muzaffarabad:** The camp is located near the campus of Prime High School, Chelabandi, a village approximately 1.5 km from the Muzaffarabad bus stand. The camp consists of a three-storey building and is used for training, communication, holding cadres as well as for other miscellaneous official purposes.
- **Markaz Syedna Bilal, Muzaffarabad:** This camp is used for imparting training to JeM terrorists. It is located on Qila Road opposite the Red Fort in Muzaffarabad city. It accommodates 50–100 operatives and functions as a transit camp for militants, prior to their infiltration into Jammu & Kashmir, with training reportedly provided by the Pakistan Army's Special Services Group (SSG) commandos. The camp comprises 5–6 constructions of various sizes.

- **Sensa Camp, Kotli District, PoK:** This camp is used by almost all outfits operating in PoK including JeM. The camp is used for giving refresher courses on various techniques to negotiate border fencing. A replica of the border fencing has been erected on the premises to impart this training.
- **Dungi Camp:** JeM has a launching detachment in Dungi, which is being used by other outfits as well, for training. It also serves as a holding camp. The camp is located at a distance of approximately 1 km north of Dungi, on the northern side of the Kotli-Dungi Road. It has buildings and barracks, a firing range, a helipad and a mosque, and is surrounded by a boundary wall.

Launching hubs of JeM in Pak/PoK
Hunty
Kel
Dudniyal
Leepa
Forward Kahuta
Kotli
Bhimber
Sialkot, Punjab

On 16 December 2017, JeM re-established a holding camp/launching detachment at Chahi Road in Samani, district Bhimber (PoJK). Earlier, JeM had its launching hub located at the main market in Samani, which was closed after surgical strikes by the Indian Army. The new hub is at a distance of approximately 5 km from Samani Bazar. One Abu Talha, who is a resident of Bhimber, is in-charge of this hub.

Prominent JeM-linked training camps/centres in Pakistan

S.No	Name of Camp	Location/Address
1	Bahawalpur Complex	Punjab, Pakistan
2	Balakot Camp	Mansehra, KPK
3	Chelabandi Camp	Muzaffarabad, PoK
4	Markaz Usman-o-Ali	Railway Link Road, near Sabaz Zar Shaadi Hall, PO Box No.15 GPO, Bahawalpur
5	Jamiat Al Noor	Mufti Wali Hasan Town, via Afghan Camp, near Seepz Park, Karachi
6	Madrasa Sunnan Bin Salma	Gaun Jogiyan, Ghadi Aslam Shop, Area Tarnab Farm, Peshawar
7	Markaz Afzal Guru Shaheed	Saryab Road, Zeeshan Town, Maulana Petrol Pump Wali Gate, Quetta

Other JeM-linked training camps/centres in Pakistan

S. No	Name of Camp	Location/Address
1	Jamia Islamia Taleem ul Quran Markazi Masjid	Khaigala Adda, Tehsil Rawalakot, district Poonch
2	Markaz Al Jameel Al Islami	Dhok Makhan Road, near Motorway Chowk, Chungi No. 26, Islamabad
3	Masjid Ayesha	Gulshan Iqbal Town, R.Y. Khan
4	Jamia Darul Uloom Taleem ul Quran	District Bagh, PoK
5	Markaz Syed Ahmad Shaheed	Balakot Road, Jaba, District Mansehra, KPK
6	Jamia Masjid Rasheed	Karachi
7	Madrisa Awais-e-Qarn (jihadi training)	
8	Jamia Masjid Rasheed	Karachi
9	Haripur Training Centre, (arms training)	Punjab

The main armed/jihadi training facility is still at Balakot, Mansehra (Markaz Saeed Ahmad Shaheed, Balakot, Mansehra, Khyber Pakhtunkhwa). There are also Askari (military) training camps located in the Jamrud area of KPK. These training camps provide ideological indoctrination and military-style guerrilla training to JeM cadres. These camps offer training to other terrorists (including members of the Taliban and other foreign mujahideen) engaged in terrorist activities in Afghanistan. The camp is located at 7–8 kms ahead of Attar-Sheesha-Balakot Road, 3 km from a signboard that reads "Madrasa Asassia Rizia Ul Tala Anha", with an arrow pointing towards the training centre, Attar-Sheesha. This markaz used to train 600-1,000 cadres in a year in different batches. The trainees include a majority from KPK, as well as a number of Afghan nationals.

Markaz Taleem-ul-Quran located in the premises of the Balakot camp, also hosts a number of Afghan students who are undergoing jihadi religious courses, primary to higher level. Children of "mujahideen" killed in various operations in Afghanistan and J&K, form a major group among these students. After completion of the requisite physical and armed training course at the markaz, cadres selected for Afghanistan operations are sent to JeM's advanced military training centre near Jamrud, Peshawar, to train in artillery and heavy weapons (LMG, rocket launchers, mortars, etc.), and are then infiltrated into Afghanistan. This Askari (military) training camp in Jamrud, KPK, is also being used to recruit youths from the area for terrorist operations in Afghanistan, particularly in the Jalalabad and Kabul regions.

JeM often conducts special "Artillery Firing Practice" for its cadres and the Taliban, in the hilly terrain just before Jamrud. Involvement of these markaz in the JeM's terrorist operations in Afghanistan was further corroborated, after the arrest of two JeM cadres by Afghan National Security Force (ANSF) in January 2019, in the Nangarhar province, while they were en route to Kabul from Jalalabad. They were tasked to conduct surveillance operations targeting Indian interests in Kabul especially, and Jalalabad, for terror attacks. These cadres also revealed that they were associated with the Peshawar set-up of JeM, and had undergone jihadi training at JeM's Markaz Usman-o-Ali in Bahawalpur, and in JeM's military centre in Balakot, Mansehra,

Pakistan. It was further revealed that they were paid monthly salaries through a JeM centre at Jamrud, KPK, Pakistan.

The general training schedule at the camps consists of:

- **Advanced Training:** After completion of the four months' basic training, 10–15 selected cadres are imparted further training in GPS handling by special trainers. They are also taught map reading, IED making, internet and computer handling.
- **Firing Practice:** During the last week of training, cadres are taken to a firing range for practice in various weapons including PIKA, AK-47 (50 rounds each), pistol and grenade.

In general, these are the main courses for jihadis:

- **Daura-e-Tarbiyah:** 7–15 days' course. The selected cadre for fidayeen are primarily motivated/indoctrinated to become fidayeen. A type of prayer or supplication called Munazat-e-Sabri, is also taught.
- **Daura-e-Tafseer or interpretation of the Quran, Daura Tafseer Ayat al Jihad:** A 40-day course. It is based on the 600 jihadi verses of Quran, as well as jihad and Qatal Fi Sabeel Allah, which translates to "fighting in the path of God".
- **Daura-e-Asasiyah or foundation course:** A 14–15 day course, this is based on three books—*Taleem-ul-Islam*, *Talem-ul-Jehad* and *Tarikh-e-Islam*.
- **Armed training courses:** Selected cadres from the basic courses are sent for fidayeen/Askari (military) training for a period of eight months to a year.
- **Daura-e-Zarar:** This course lasts for a duration of 40 days. Cadres are given training in the handling of pistols, AK-47, LMG, rocket launchers, UBGL and grenades, as well as weapons and communication.

- **Daura-e-Al Araad:** This course has a duration of four months. Cadres are given training in handling of pistol, AK-47, LMG, rocket launcher, UBGL, grenades, religious training, lessons on weapons, communication, and are also given firing practice for ten days.

According to local sources, the Nangarhar province in Afghanistan has been virtually ceded by the Taliban to Jaish-e-Mohammed. A fair number of training camps are located in the area—the very same camps that Bill Roggio once called "peace training camps". Some camps are still Taliban-run and house only small delegations of JeM members, while the so-called Mustaquir camps that have been contracted out to Masood Azhar and company for the JeM, are in the majority here. The handover of the para-military facilities to the Pakistani terrorist group is just the latest act in a long and fruitful collaboration established for years now, between the Taliban, the Haqqanis and the Jaish-e-Mohammed. These are groups that even children in the area know of by now. The Jaish-e-Mohammed, remote-controlled by ISI, has in the past, provided the Taliban with an uninterrupted flow of Pakistani recruits from the ex-FATA (Federally Administered Tribal Areas), Khyber Pakhtunkhwa, and even the Punjab. The Balakot training camp predominantly housed recruits ready to be sent to Afghanistan. Azhar and his people also provided a considerable number of suicide bombers to both the Taliban and the Haqqani Network. And now they are collecting credit, being aided and sheltered when necessary by the "interim government" of Afghanistan

According to local sources, the bulk of JeM cadres have been transferred to Nangarhar, on ISI instructions from the Khyber Agency, and to Pan Chinar on the Pakistan-Afghanistan border.

JeM, i.e., ISI, covers all maintenance and logistical expenses of the camps, including the salaries of instructors and workers. The camps, particularly in the Khogiyani district, are almost all located near villages or civilian settlements, and have every necessary amenity. There are hostels for trainees, residences for instructors, madrasas, mosques, classrooms, and camps for drills. Some are even said to have swimming pools. In contrast, the organisation's cadres stay in separate camps, which they apparently share with senior civil servants. The training programme for new recruits includes physical training, classroom lectures, dismantling and cuffing of weapons, and handling of weapons and ammunition. However, shooting practice is carried out away from the camp, because of the proximity to civilian settlements. Apparently, recruits have a full range of weapons—AK-47s, LMGs, rocket launchers, grenades, explosives, and anything else that is part of the petty terrorist handbook.

Students also attend jungle survival courses held in the Kunar forest. The best ones are then directed to a specific training programme for terrorists to be infiltrated into Kashmir, and according to Indian intelligence, there is a cell of infiltrated cadres in J&K coming right from Nangarhar. In addition to routine teachings, the master's programme for particularly gifted terrorists includes a ten-day intensive course that includes subjects such as breaking into military camps, camouflage, concealment, survival techniques, and IED fabrication. Students are also taken to areas that replicate the terrain of areas such as Neelam, Sharda or Kotli (in India's J&K) to hone their terrain knowledge and contingency management.

Supervision of the Nangarhar camps is entrusted to Abdul Rauf Asghar Kashmiri, Masood Azhar's brother and the organisation's military commander. He is the same individual, just to give the reader a quick summary, who supervised the Balakot camp and provided an impressive number of recruits to the Taliban over the past years. Rauf Azhar or Asgar as he is also known, despite being placed in protective custody at one point, has been seen over and over repeatedly, in the cheerful company of ISKP figures. Notably, a few months before the Taliban entered Kabul, Rauf Azhar had accompanied his brother Masood Azhar to Islamabad to meet with their patrons. The visit was to discuss, it is said, about the role of JeM in the months ahead. It appears that during that meeting, there was a bit of a tiff between old comrades. Indeed, ISI argued that Azhar and his people should temporarily abandon Kashmir, and instead focus on Afghanistan by providing both financial and logistical support to the Taliban. According to Rauf Azhar, the goals could be easily pursued in tandem, and the synergy between the two would reinvigorate troop morale. The ISI line prevailed by a whisker. In the same months, JeM, in addition to the Lashkar-e-Toiba and other Pakistani terrorist groups, had been busy raising funds for the Taliban, and facilitating the movements of jihadis, including Al Qaida members, between Pakistan and Afghanistan. The rest, is history.

After the Taliban and Haqqanis took Kabul, Masood Azhar and Rauf Azhar could focus again on their main target—Kashmir. Infiltration, according to the Indian Army, then resumed in a big way. The Srinagar province had been the scene of no small amount of violence. Afghanistan, whatever the Americans may think, has never ceased to be a giant hub for various terrorist organisations. Now, with a government of terrorists, it was certainly not going to get any better. No one should forget that there is not only Al Qaida or ISIS, there are other organisations as well. And JeM and the Lashkar-e-Toiba are not local organisations, neither are they acting only against India—both have a global jihadi agenda to which, perhaps, it would be good to pay attention.

The worst was yet to come. Especially because of late, terrorists have been found to be using highly sophisticated weapons, what was left behind by NATO forces and smuggled from Afghanistan for the use of the Pakistani-based and Pakistani "baked" groups. In particular, in 2024, the Indian SF recovered a number of M4 series rifles in various operations carried out in J&K. A 2024 *India Today* report cited intelligence, stating that ISI officials and terror commanders in Pakistan-occupied Kashmir (PoK) planned to supply M4s for attacks in India. In July of the same year, the same SF recovered from terrorists neutralised in Kupwara district, an Austrian-origin Steyr Augustine (AUG) rifle—the kind of rifle notably being actively used by Pakistani SSG in their inventories.

It is worth noting here that M4 rifles were used in the 22 April 2025 Pahalgam attack by the terrorists, and it suggests grim possibilities about the attack's planning, sponsorship, and execution. The M4 is in fact a US-designed, lightweight, gas-operated assault rifle, widely used by military and special forces, notably the US Army and by the Special Service Group, as well as elite units of the Pakistani Army. Its possession and use indicates access to advanced, military-grade weaponry, suggesting either direct or indirect support from a state or non-state actor with access to such equipment.

SRINAGAR IS STILL BEAUTIFUL

'Mon amour, Srinagar is still beautiful, although full of soldiers and shaken by yesterday's attack. Tonight they destroyed part of it with explosives to flush out the Jaish-e-Mohammad militants who were inside. The number of dead increased. This morning I entered the still smoldering parliament and did interviews. I also got the views of ordinary people. There were more attacks by the Jaish, joint with the Harkat ul Mujaheddin.'

My husband, the late Sergio Trippodo, author of a book on Kashmir published in Italy by Editori Riuniti, entered Srinagar the morning of 2 October 2001. While he was still on the train, JeM attacked the Srinagar Assembly. It was difficult back then, without cell phones and with very erratic internet connections, to stay in touch. Most of the time, phone lines were mute and you could never be sure your emails were going through. So I was managing from Italy, forwarding his articles and maintaining contact with radios and TV channels. He sent me pictures (printed on the spot and sent by courier) of the attack's aftermath—pictures of devastating brutality, but just a prelude to what would happen later.

The first suicide terrorist attack in the Valley was conducted by JeM within a few months of the formation of the terrorist group. On 19 April 2000, a suicide car bomb exploded outside the Indian Army's 15 Corp headquarters in Badami Bagh, Srinagar. This was the first "VBIED" attack in which two soldiers were killed. Then on 1 October 2001, JeM terrorists were responsible for a car bomb targeting the State Assembly building in Srinagar. The militants entered the building and engaged in a shootout with Indian Security Forces, leaving 31 killed and six wounded. This attack was a wake-up call to the rest of the world that was busy with Afghanistan, the Twin Towers attack and operation "Enduring Freedom", and who were underestimating the danger in front of them. From an article Sergio wrote for *Limes—Italian Review of Geopolitics* in 2001:

> Another area that at first the Durable Freedom coalition did not want to consider is the eastern border, where India and Pakistan have been fighting since independence over the thorny issue of Kashmir. Two days before the attack on Afghanistan, and three days after the bombing of the parliament in Srinagar, British Prime Minister Tony Blair had traveled to Islamabad and Delhi to discuss the issue. But by the end of the meetings he had declared that Kashmir was a secondary issue that would be taken care of "later." In the days that followed, at the same time as the air raids, Indian troops massed along the Kargil front in preparation for firefights that were to take place shortly thereafter. Pro-bin Laden militants of the Jaish-e-Mohammed, perpetrators of the October 1 Srinagar attack, and the Harkat-ul-Mujahidin carried out joint actions in Indian territory from their bases in Pakistan. Then the popular outcry against the attacks in Afghanistan erupted, and that of the Indian government against the United States to which Delhi demanded

to expand the fight against international terrorism to Kashmir by first banning the Jaish-e-Mohammed. The latest request was not granted until mid-October, but the Jaish took precaution by immediately changing its name to "Tehrik-ul-Furkhan" while Washington responded by sending Colin Powell to Delhi and Islamabad to re-discuss the issue. A visit that was met by heavy Indian shelling, the first after ten months of relative calm, which destroyed eleven positions located in Pakistani territory. It is not yet known what the repercussions will be in the other countries indirectly involved in the Kashmiri issue, Nepal and Bangladesh, but it is certain that even this outbreak was underestimated by the strategists of Enduring Freedom.

And, a year later:
As attention focuses on Afghanistan, the Kashmiri issue escalates. A week before air raids against the Taliban and Al Qaida, the Srinagar parliament is stormed by Jaish-e-Muhammad guerrillas. The imminent start of Operation Enduring Freedom overshadows the serious attack. It underestimates the fact that Afghanistan, Pakistan and Kashmir have already for years formed an axis along which all the major Islamic fundamentalist groups in the region move and operate. Not even on Dec. 13, when an Islamic commando carried out another attack against the parliament in New Delhi, does the international coalition realize that Kashmir is a high-risk area because it balances what is happening in Afghanistan and because it is a disputed territory between two nuclear powers. Only British Prime Minister Tony Blair makes a fleeting appearance in Islamabad and New Delhi. Little leaks out of the intervening talks except that "for Kashmir we will see later." As if the Kashmiri powder keg can be defused at will

and addressed when it suits the Enduring Freedom coalition most. Presumably, the disinterest in that hot zone was then dictated by the assumption that the one in Afghanistan would be a flash war. Instead, the evidence of facts has shown that the Afghanistan, Pakistan and Kashmir axis has functioned as an excellent defense tool for the Taliban and al-Qā'ida. About a year after the attack on the United States, the difference is that the fundamentalist needle has shifted to the east, involving Pakistan and consequently Kashmir more, without leaving the Western front free. At this point, India, continually threatened by the infiltration of the Kashmiri and Afghan mujāhidīn as well as affected by their guerrilla operations, begins to put its foot down and masses troops along the border with Pakistan. Another conflict between the two arch-rivals looms, and this time concern that it will cross over into a nuclear war alarms the superpowers. Top U.S. and British policymakers take turns in Delhi and Islamabad but it seems too late to find a negotiated solution. Thus a modern as well as dangerous form of deterrence is resorted to: making even conventional conflict so risky as to frustrate its implementation. Therefore, many countries that form the international coalition, and which are also the world's largest arms producers, reinforce the flow of substantial military aid to Pakistan and India. Economic priorities and the game of alliances becomes less clear. The most cautious in these trades is, strange to say, the Bush administration. Between June and July 2002, the United States delays delivery of helicopter gunships and F-16 fighter jets to Pakistan, while the State Department gets into conflict with the Pentagon over Awacs anti-missile systems and Falcon spy planes that Israel would like to sell to India. Thus it is Russia, India's habitual supplier, that sells Mi-71 military helicopters to Pakistan. For its part, Britain continues to supply arms to both Asian countries even as it withdraws "for security reasons" its diplomats from the region. Meanwhile, China is accused by the United States of failing to respect the principle of equidistance in international counterterrorism scenarios and playing a dangerous role in Asia's geostrategic balances. In this game, each government denies or defends itself as best it can, but it is clear that political and diplomatic arrangements fail to curb the drive for unbridled proliferation in the region, much less find a solution to the Kashmiri issue. On the contrary, the lack of synergy between international politics and economic interests only exacerbates it. Indeed, it is unlikely that two enemy nations, having received billions of dollars in armaments and military aid in a matter of months, will not make use in the more or less distant future of the war potential placed at their disposal. Just as it is also doubtful that the "strategy of deterrence" adopted so far will forever avert a nuclear conflict. The Kashmiri problem, and the consequent stabilization of the Indian subcontinent, thus remains an open question that demands to be resolved.

For years Sergio, Beniamino Natale, I, and a few other analysts, made a round of the TV channels and radio, trying to explain that Al Qaida was not the only or the more dangerous terrorist group in the region, and that Pakistan, and not Afghanistan, was the real threat. A threat not only to India but to the rest of the world. Many years later, a famous Pakistani journalist who was often called to USA for briefings, told me from exasperation: 'I don't know if they are really dumb or just pretend to be.' And an even more famous American general whose name I don't want to quote because the conversation was not on record, after a conference, replied angrily at my remarks: 'What do you want us to do, bomb Pakistan? Pakistan is a nuclear country!' During all these years, the narrative had not changed that much. Srinagar, the Srinagar we used to love so much, changed a lot thanks to Jaish-e-Mohammed and their Pakistani handlers. Again, as Sergio had written, it was still beautiful, but this time, shaken to its very core. A lost paradise.

When you arrived in Srinagar once upon a time, the signs said "Welcome to Paradise on Earth". A paradise of lakes nestled among vegetation and forests, of apple trees that perfumed the air. A paradise of mountains and valleys and plains, of saffron and raisins, of embroidered shawls of fine wool. A paradise sung about since ancient times by poets and writers, also called "the Switzerland of India", a favourite location for years, for song and dance numbers in many Bollywood films. A favourite summer vacation destination for kings and usurpers, tourists and travellers, hippies and spiritual seekers. When you arrived in Srinagar, you used to go swimming in the Dal Lake, live in a house boat, shop at the floating market of shikaras.... In the city, you could go to find Hindu pandits explaining Tantra or you could instead sit with devout Muslims inside a mosque listening to sermons. You could have gone to visit what legend has it is the tomb of Christ—venerated and revered by all, right next to the tomb of a local Sufi saint.

When you arrived in Srinagar, later, in the days of hatred, you wondered if paradise would ever return—you doubted whether it had ever existed. The Pandits were no more, hunted in the 1990s by terrorists who have been trying for years to Islamise a fundamentally secular state. A hundred thousand people were forced to flee from their burned homes. Many had been killed, women raped, terrified children still bear the marks, after years of persecution, house boats fell into disrepair for lack of customers. On the streets, more than stalls, you saw barbed wire and sandbags.

When you arrived in Srinagar in the days of hatred, it felt like a different city. The curfew had emptied the streets and sealed the shutters of stores; the gates of houses and cottages were barred. On street corners, soldiers in combat gear guarded the emptiness that at any moment could once again resound with screams and explosions. On the walls, black writings stood out calling for freedom, "We want freedom" and declaring "We are not with India". The streets filled up only intermittently, not with children playing or worshippers going to prayer or women crowding the market, but with demonstrators. They were filled with stones and cries of hatred, which become at times an all-against-all that left no one standing. For Kashmir, the immense region it once was and which proudly brought together within a common culture people belonging to different religions and ethnicities, has been fragmented and dismembered both politically and geographically, to be reduced in the collective imagination, to the Srinagar Valley alone—to a geopolitical "issue", the so-called "Kashmir issue". It became a privileged hub for terrorists.

As Praveen Swami wrote in 2002 for *Frontline*:

After the U.S. bombing of Afghanistan began, the group's plans crystallised. Western tourists in New Delhi's downmarket Paharganj area were to be bombed as a reprisal for the killing of Al Qaeda cadre. Cash, weapons and explosives were taken to Jammu, while other consignments were moved to New Delhi. The group planned to bomb the MLAs' Hostel in Jammu, and then escape by using Wani's car to reach the airport. Their first attempt to set off an explosion in Jammu failed, and the group missed their Jet Airways flight to New Delhi. A travel agent was then told to make bookings for a few days later – but their arrest made sure the tickets were never used. What Ayub's arrest makes clear is that terrorist groups in Jammu and Kashmir are in the process of restructuring themselves in significant ways. While the relationship between HuM elements and the Al Qaeda is not new – one-time HuM and now Jaish-e-Mohammad head Masood Azhar studied with Taliban chief Mohammad Omar at the Binori seminary in Karachi – no operational collaboration has been seen in the past. After its eviction from Afghanistan, the Al Qaeda presumably wishes to deploy some of its assets in India, using the HuM's network. As further arrests follow, a clearer picture of this network should emerge. There are enough dots on [the] page, however, to be certain the picture that will emerge will not be a pretty one.

And no, it wasn't "pretty". After the Srinagar State Assembly attack on 13 December 2001, the JeM along with LeT, attacked the Parliament building in Delhi, killing nine people. Here is a list of just the major attacks:

- On 2 November 2005, JeM carried out a suicide car bomb attack outside the home of the outgoing Chief Minister, Mufti Mohammad Sayeed, near Srinagar, killing seven civilians including a ten-year-old boy and three police officers.
- On 20 March 2015, a fidayeen squad of terrorists in army fatigues stormed a police station on the Jammu-Pathankot National Highway, killing five persons, including three security force personnel and two civilians, while ten others were injured. A note written in Urdu was recovered from the encounter site, which indicated the terrorists' affiliation with JeM. Leads verified the role of the Pakistani terror group in the attack.
- In November 2015, three JeM terrorists attacked an army

camp leading to a fire in the oil dump and barracks. One JCO and a civilian were killed, while all the three JeM terrorists were eliminated in the ensuing encounter.

- On 2 January 2016, the Air Force base in Pathankot, Punjab was attacked by terrorists linked to the JeM group. Four terrorists were neutralised by the NSG. Arms and ammunition were recovered from the dead terrorists. Investigative and operational inputs established that the attack was planned and executed by the JeM with the help of the ISI.

There was a spurt in JeM attacks, particularly post the Pathankot attack (January 2016) in the Valley. Synergy among the different terror outfits was also seen in the Valley, with an increased sharing of resources and coordination on the ground, for executing attacks. Handlers/militant operatives have been successful in luring/motivating a substantial number of Kashmiri youth to join the tanzeem locally. I have presented a non-exhaustive list of the major attacks in Chapter 4, that show an increase in terrorist activity in that period, which are important in this context as well.

I was in Srinagar a number of times during those years, and wrote a number of reports during those visits. This is what I wrote back in 2010 after returning from the Valley, amid what was called the "intifada". Although it was described as a "spontaneous" protest, I witnessed firsthand how carefully orchestrated and controlled it actually was. I personally sat with Syed Ali Shah Gilani, who probably thought I was some kind of dumb foreign lady ready to swallow any kind of farcical information and distortion of history and events. He did not even bother to go into another room when a couple of guys came to report to him about the riots of the night before. The gentleman,

I recall, was very annoyed by my questions. He started on a patronising note, addressing me as "beta" and even explaining to me what "beta" meant. He was livid when I left. It is really not worth it to reproduce the entirety of the interview which was published in *Limes—Italian Review of Geopolitics*, an interview full of propaganda and nothing else, but this was my report:

The facts, summarized briefly, are these: last June 11, a tear gas canister fired at the crowd by the Srinagar police, hit a 17-year-old boy, Mohammad Husain Matoo, in the head, killing him. The boy was returning home from school, and his death was completely unrelated to the protests. His death, and those of other boys (88 to date) who have been declared martyrs and died in similar circumstances, have been used by protesters as flags to wave in the eyes of the crowd to arouse further resentment against New Delhi. The protests in the streets of Srinagar, saw groups of very young people fighting the army with stones. These have been going on for a few months now, fomented by any pretext, whether serious or not. And they have been likened by many, Pakistan foremost, to an "intifada made in Kashmir", spontaneously born out of local people's anger at the Delhi government, and a resurgence after a long lull, of separatist movements and jihad in the disputed state.

Bands of barely teenage boys confront the army with stones. They are the children of the petty bourgeoisie, children of a class with no prospects and no future that cultivates anger and dreams, becoming easy prey for those who speculate on these dreams and anger. 'A lethal vicious cycle has now been set in motion,' declares a person very close to the region's government, who however, does not want his name to appear. 'The army and police are not trained in crowd control and do not even have the proper equipment. They have been fighting jihad for 30 years. All they know is to react by opening fire.' And each new "martyr" plays into the hands of the puppet masters who pull the strings from their own living rooms. With each new martyr, more protests are triggered. And a new curfew, which means closed schools and stores. Government schools and small businesses, the small businesses run by the very parents of those protesting. The schools attended by the children who are on the streets and are in danger of growing up without any education. And who are beginning to turn to the madrasas financed with Saudi and Pakistani money that have been springing up like mushrooms for some time in a place, Kashmir, traditionally the cradle of liberal, enlightened Islam. Slowly changing the deep cultural fabric of the region and signalling the momentous change taking place at the top echelons of power in Srinagar and in the modes of separatist struggle.

The senior leader of the All Parties Hurriyat Conference, Syed Ali Gilani, has been providing the young protesters with a "road map" of the protest for months. He organizes lockouts and demonstrations, and receives young people who go daily to report on developments in the streets. Gilani, of Wahabi denomination and a supporter of Kashmir's right to self-determination, insists that: 'Pakistan and militant organizations have no role in this. The youth are not armed by Pakistan or other nations across the border, they are unarmed and peaceful. They are victims of the brutal methods of Indian police shooting at unarmed boys and children.' However, the last time Gilani called a peaceful demonstration, there were eighteen deaths, several government buildings were set on fire, and a number of Christian schools were stormed. The truth is that not even old Gilani can control the crowd anymore, and in one of his last public appearances, he received his fair share of stones thrown at the car he was travelling in. The event has been crowd manoeuvred, however, by a new terror network that moves the ranks behind the scenes and seeks to secure succession to the leadership of the separatists. Protagonists of this new course are Aasya Andrabi, founder and chairwoman of the Dukhtaran-e-Millat (the only female jihadi group) and her husband Muhammad bin Qasim, once commander of the Jamait-ul-Mujahideen terrorist organization and now a member of the Muslim League. Qasim has been in prison for years, but that is not stopping him from running for the leadership role in the succession to the now 82-year-old Gilani.

However, Aasya and Qasim have different objectives from that of the old leader. They are fighting for the establishment of an Islamic state of Kashmir that would merge with Pakistan. And for this, they are funded and supported by the Hizbul Mujahiddin and the Lashkar-e-Toiba, which at present are not operating on their own, or at least not openly in Srinagar, but are promoting "spontaneous" protests by local teenagers. The change is no small one, and it is likely to have very heavy repercussions. The so-called "Kashmir issue" has, in fact, always been a primarily political problem and has been addressed as such, even by the Islamic fundamentalist organizations infiltrated from across the border. However, Aasya, Qasim, and their followers are gradually turning it into a religious issue by indoctrinating young boys with fundamentalist Islamic values. Aasya, by her own admission, divides the world into Muslims and non-Muslims. Her 18-year-old son Khurram was prevented from playing cricket for the Indian youth national team because, according to his parents, "He was born to serve Islam" and destined to be "the next Osama bin Laden."

The Talibanization of a part of Srinagar, particularly downtown, a section now effectively cut off from the rest of the city by an invisible yet impenetrable border, is already underway. The recent assaults on Sikh communities and Christian schools are an early symptom of this. And it is likely, if not addressed soon, to turn the former "paradise on earth" into the much less paradisiacal Swat Valley. The warning signs are all there. But none of the players seem willing to act. Demagoguery and vested interests are many, too many. And the money circulating on each side of the barricades, is even more. It seems that the Kashmir issue has become an industry in itself—one that now sustains the Valley's crumbling economy. Opposition politicians are running their street squads, trying to bring down the local sitting government. Gilani has his followers, Aasya and Qasim theirs, the army and police work is assured. Children and young people are the ones who pay the price: two of the dead were as young as 11. And curiously, no human rights organization, none of those that rightly protest against the methods of the army and police, takes to the streets to protest against the ones who hide behind children and teenagers, sending them knowingly into harm's way to die as martyrs and feed a cynical political agenda.

Back then, I also had a long conversation with Aasya Andrabi's son, Khurram. Khurram's story, to me, was emblematic of what was really happening to Kashmiri youth:

Young Khurram, just turned eighteen, says he is "proud to

be the son of two great people" (both currently in jail) and completely agrees with their ideals. Which are summarized as dividing the world into Muslims and non-Muslims, and fighting for Kashmir to become part of Pakistan. The life of Khurram, who was one of the first boys to organize stone pelting against the police and army in Srinagar, has always been inextricably intertwined with the political life of his town and all of Kashmir. And he has been heavily marked, despite his young age, by the family history. Arrested with daddy and mommy while still in swaddling clothes, the boy was destined (or predestined) by his parents to be, as he himself declares, "the next Osama bin Laden", and to serve the cause for which his parents were fighting. He, in reality, wanted only one thing: to play cricket.

Selected for the youth national teams when he was 16, he was prevented from playing under India's flag. Just as he was barred from listening to music, watching movies, and reading anything other than religious books. As a result, the boy spends his days wandering in the streets doing nothing with friends and watching television channels that broadcast sports. The dream of becoming a cricket star has remained somewhere deep in his heart, bitter and sweet at the same time. Khurram and the boys like him live "downtown", a ghettoized, marginalized part of Srinagar where frustration and anger are cultivated and weaponized. You see them on the streets, confronting the police and army, armed with stones and grievances. Armed with big rocks and an anger skilfully fomented and exploited by those who see in their young lives nothing more than powerful symbols—made for headlines, footage, and the furthering of political ends.

The political star of Aasya and Qasim shines brighter than ever at this moment and is quietly but significantly causing a change. And while the full impact may not yet be visible from the outside, the transformation underway is profound. The game that has been played for months on the streets of Srinagar, in fact, is one with immoral and indecent contours for which all parties involved are responsible. The victims, increasingly, are no longer jihadi guerrillas but young boys. Two of whom, in recent months, were just 11 years old. Victims of a game bigger than themselves, in which teenage boys are sent into the streets to chant protest slogans against Delhi, and throwing stones at police and army. The police and the army, are equipped with shields and bamboo bulletproof vests, and most importantly, are trained for counter insurgency and not to handle civilian uprisings. Predictably, when they react with force—sometimes fatally—they ignite public fury and feed fresh "martyrs" to the propaganda machine. Martyrs who did not willingly choose their fate, especially at the age of eleven, who did not choose to abandon their kites and cricket bats for a sudden and precocious awakening of political consciousness. Martyrs who are manipulated by a new terror network that is rapidly taking the place of traditional jihad. A network that exploits the hopelessness of a generation—deprived of education, economic opportunity, and even a normal childhood—and shields them from a future, offering instead a cause. And which is reframing a complex political dispute such as the Kashmir issue, into a religious struggle with all its implications.

The assaults on the Sikh community last August, and now against Christian-run churches and schools, are an early symptom of this. Over the past couple of years, madrasas tied to extremist ideologies and funded by Saudi and Pakistani sources have mushroomed across the Valley. These institutions are filling the vacuum left by shuttered public schools, curfews, and economic collapse. The indoctrination at these madrasas have been at the expense of Khurram and boys like him, robbed of their dreams, deprived of a decent education because schools remain closed due to curfews and lockouts, and denied of a job because Kashmir's economy is now on its knees. Boys who will have no other option but to turn to madrasas to receive a ghost of education and to find identity and purpose in radical teachings. Boys who will sooner or later turn the Kashmir Valley into the next Swat Valley.

And this invariably happened.
Again I was in Kashmir in 2016, to witness death and destruction:
Fifty-six dead and some three thousand injured in firefights with police, thirty-three days of curfew, relations between India and Pakistan once again at rock bottom. The spark for the latest unrest was the killing by the Indian army of the twenty-two-year-old Burhan Wani. Burhan commanded a cell of militants of the Hizbul Mujahidin, a terrorist group that has been operating for years in the region, created, financed and trained more or less openly by Pakistan to sustain a low-grade war in the region. Clashes between militants and the army have become a grimly familiar part of life in Kashmir, and rarely make the headlines now. But Burhan's death was different. Indeed, as one Indian army officer who wishes to remain anonymous commented with bitter irony, the boy managed to do more damage in death, than during all his

militant career. Upon news of his death, thousands of people poured into the streets across Kashmir, throwing stones and anything within reach at the army. The military responded with the same incredible shortsightedness, which has affected its approach to civilian protests for years—opening fire on the crowd using tear gas and pellet guns. The result? Thousands of citizens, including women and young children, did not die, but were hospitalised with very serious eye damage. Many are at risk of permanent blindness. Result number two—the Indian Army managed to create a kind of Che Guevara in Islamic sauce out of a boy whom the same local intelligence called a "Facebook militant" and a "poster-boy" for parlour jihad.

The Kashmir Chief Minister Mehbooba Mufti remarked that had the soldiers known they had Burhan Wani in their sights, they might have tried to capture him alive. He was, after all, more than just another militant. Wani had become a symbol—a reflection of a deeper shift unfolding across the Kashmir Valley. The last "intifada" in the Valley was in 2011. Even then, the trigger had been the killing of a boy by security forces. And for a few months, clashes between the army and the population, mostly teenagers or so, had turned the streets into a theatre of war. Yet another.

Even back in 2011, however, analysts had warned that India's strategy of repression was dangerously counterproductive. A dangerous cycle was already in motion. Schools had been shut for long periods due to curfews. Government institutions were paralyzed. With every new protest and every new death, more schools closed, more families suffered economic losses, and more young people were pushed toward the margins creating a new generation of militants.

The new jihadis are young or very young, from good or excellent families, affluent, educated and like Wani, use the Net to recruit militants, radicalise, and glamorise the cause of militant jihad. The word of the Hizbul Mujahidin, the word of Islamabad promising "panem et circenses" to all those disillusioned with Indian politics, full of anger, and always feeling like second-class citizens in their own nation.

Unfortunately, on their skin, and on the skin of all Kashmiris, a much larger and more complex game is being played. An intelligence source, also strictly anonymous, commented, 'The killing of Wani was a glaring mistake that we would never have made. We walked into a trap laid by the Pakistanis—and we fell for it.'

By then, the jihadi business had started to bloom once again, amplified by social media. Social media recruitment and indoctrination had become the new normal. All groups starting from JeM, had their own platforms for indoctrination and radicalisation of Kashmiri youth. Usually, hard-core stone-pelters and over ground workers (OGW) are the potential soft targets who have been motivated by terrorist operatives and handlers to join the group. The playbook was well-established. Kashmiri youths were encouraged to sneak illegally into Pakistan/PoJK through the LoC, or to cross the border on valid documents to receive military and terror training. Thereafter, they were sent back across the border to operate in the Valley—either to fight directly against Indian security forces or to serve as logistical facilitators for terror networks. As a local source declared:

Training of cadres at various active camps of JeM outfits located in PoJK and Pakistan is a regular affair. These cadres, after training, are launched into J&K through active launching hubs located in the bordering areas with specific briefs. These launching hubs are located generally close to LoC/IB for facilitating the reconnaissance of the terrain to be used for infiltration, and to carry out BAT/snipping action on Indian Security Forces (ISFs) along the IB.

JeM recruits are indoctrinated at Bahawalpur, Pakistan and are then sent to Peshawar for training to successfully infiltrate into J&K from launching hubs along Neelam Valley, PoJK and Rajouri-Poonch-Jammu areas, particularly from the Shakargarh sector of Pakistan. Apart from jihadi lectures and training in arms and ammunition, cadres are made to train in infiltration, jungle survival, high altitude acclimatisation and snow trekking, crossing rivers, fence cutting, GPS training, etc. Once the group is stationed at their launching hubs, the following are the points kept in mind for infiltrating into J&K. After reporting at the launching hub, the cadres are familiarised with the border area and terrain, by conducting reconnaissance along with local guides. The in-charges of launching hubs and local guides have close liaison with the concerned company commanders of the Pakistan Army and Pakistan Rangers deployed at the border. They are in charge of exploration of gaps and routes for infiltration, and are supposed to maintain communication with senior command and the local Army and Rangers, who are deployed to receive the group for further movement in the hinterland. And, at the opportune time, the group, equipped with all the necessary items for navigation, is infiltrated into Indian territory.

What we were witnessing was not just another wave of unrest but the systematic replacement of a political conflict with a religious insurgency, carefully planned, funded, and executed from across the border. And its victims—boys like Wani, and many even younger, were being cultivated from childhood to serve as fodder for someone else's war. Conventionally, infiltration would take place in the summer season. However, lately, terrorists have tried to infiltrate even during the winter season by using special snow clothing and equipment. There has been a considerable shift of terrorists from the LoC to the International Border (IB) for infiltration.

The IB has been favourable due to presence of paddy fields. The infiltrating cadres, take advantage of the long grass along the IB for infiltration. While the LoC region of the J&K is mountainous, comprising of forests and snow-clad peaks during winters, the IB region is largely plain. The mountainous region, ridges, rivers and gaps, make a safe passage for infiltration. Fencing on such terrain is a difficult task. Infiltration is also done through tunnels along the IB, particularly in the Samba and Hira Nagar areas of J&K. These tunnels are utilised mainly for infiltration, and for the supply of arms and ammunition.

Sandbags recovered from one such tunnel had manufacture markings engraved of Karachi, indicating the handiwork of the Pakistani establishment. This was reportedly used for pushing JeM terrorist cadres into J&K, from the Shakargarh area. The possibility of the existence of similar tunnels on IB in the Kathua and Samba districts for infiltration of terrorist cadres, along with the smuggling of arms and ammunition, cannot be ruled out say experts. Pakistan-based terror outfits, especially JeM, have been seen intensifying the supply of arms and ammunition (including M4 rifles) from across the LoC/IB. In this process, the use of drones for dropping weapons close to IB, especially in the Jammu, Samba and Rajouri sectors, has come to notice. Since June 2020, there have been at least 46 instances of drone dropping or sightings in Jammu and the adjoining Punjab sectors, respectively. The same month of June that year, two low intensity IEDs were dropped from a suspected drone near the hanger of the Air Force Technical Area Satwari, Jammu (Jammu Airport), which was the handiwork of the Pakistan-based JeM/LeT operatives. This is what I was writing in 2019, just before another turning point:

> At first glance, the discovery of two dead militants in an orchard in Anantnag, Kashmir, on the afternoon of 26 June seemed like yet another routine chapter in the long, grim chronicle of violence in the Valley: one of the men, Adil Ahmed Das, was dead; the other, Arif Bhat, was dying. Das bore gunshot wounds and signs of strangulation: to kill him they used the string that held his pants. In Kashmir, such killings rarely register as news. Police operations are nearly daily occurrences, and the appearance of slain militants is sadly not unusual. Yet, this incident was different. While some sites and some Telegram channels attribute the death of Das to the Indian armed forces, other channels and other sites suggested otherwise. Uncontrolled rumours were beginning to circulate, until a Pakistani analyst working for the British think-tank Aurora Intel, Faran Jeffery, managed to piece together a story with some disturbing implications. Das had recently abandoned the ranks of the Lashkar-e-Toiba to join Islamic State's Hind Province (ISHP), a group affiliated with ISIS. Two of his former comrades called him, they told him that they wanted to change sides too. After taking photos with him to document their supposed allegiance to ISHP, they coldly executed him and seized his weapons. 'It was

only a matter of time before this happened,' Jeffery commented. 'Until now, rival terrorist groups stationed in Kashmir have avoided any direct confrontation with each other, because they were busy fighting against the Indian army. And this episode can potentially precipitate Kashmir into a full-blown civil war between fighting groups.' If confirmed, the implications are deeply unsettling. For decades, militancy in Kashmir has been dominated by groups like Hizbul Mujahidin and Lashkar-e-Toiba—armed, funded, and directed by Pakistan's state and non-state apparatus. But over the past few years, the landscape has shifted.

The Islamic State Jammu & Kashmir, or the ISJK, a group that emerged in the late 2010s, which claimed responsibility for this particular attack, and which previously had only a few members, is steadily gaining ground. So is the United Jihad Council, which is based in Pakistan but has major ideological differences both with the "traditional" groups and with Gilani's Hurriyat in Srinagar. A few days ago, yet another small group of budding terrorists swore an oath of loyalty to Al-Baghdadi, from Kashmir. They released a video in which they stated: 'We have succeeded in founding a jihadi group based on the uniqueness of Allah and destroying the foundations of nationalism, democracy and self-determination, we have declared war on these concepts. We do not fight for Kashmir, ours is a war of faith.' The same war of faith that other organizations affiliated to the Islamic State, such as the Islamic State Khorasan Province, are fighting in the province of Kunar in Afghanistan against the Taliban, aided by members of the Lashkar-e-Toiba.

In addition to the Islamic State of Hind Khorasan (ISHK) and ISJK, other groups in Kashmir are also fighting the jihadis of Ansar Ghazwatul Hind, a group affiliated to Al Qaeda. For the umpteenth time, the very Frankenstein created by Pakistan's decades-long patronage of militancy is now mutating beyond its control. It is no secret to anyone that ISI and the Pakistani army in Afghanistan have been playing on several tables for some time now, and that some sections of the affiliates of the Islamic State are also dependent on Pakistan. This strategy is now unravelling. Just as a faction of the Taliban became uncontrollable over a decade ago, so too are portions of the Islamic State affiliates, now operating with growing independence and ideological zeal. Years and years of indoctrination of young Kashmiris by LeT and HM have borne fruit, but for India, they are poisoned fruits.

In recent years, the closure of public schools on the occasion of increasingly frequent disorders has given a free hand to madrasas and mullahs. Social media does the rest. Just take a tour on Telegram to find yourself in the eye of a storm of propaganda full of contradiction and without control. A war between jihadi groups is a war, first of all, on the shoulders of the Kashmiris: if the "new" groups no longer fight for Kashmir but for the supremacy of the Islamic State, the "old" groups as well as a good chunk of ordinary citizens oppose the project. And while the United Jihad Council calls for the unity of fighters, those belonging to the new groups have no intention of responding. Indeed, they swear revenge for the death of Das.

Of course, the Indian army could stand in the front row armed with popcorn, watching the jihadis slaughter one another, but it is not a good idea since Kashmir risks being turned into a powder keg. No one knows, and it is very difficult to predict what will happen in the coming days or months. But what will happen in Kashmir is in many ways linked to the Afghan situation. The repercussions of the struggle between rival groups and state-sponsors could be greater, much greater than what the West imagines or manages to predict.

After Balakot, under renewed international pressure, particularly from the Financial Action Task Force (FATF) and Asia Pacific Group (APG), as well as developments following the Balakot Air Strike (26 February 2019), the Pakistan government claimed to be taking action against terror groups in their country, including the Jaish-e-Mohammed (JeM). These actions included claims of taking over properties, monitoring of activities, and detention of senior functionaries and cadres. Further, the Pakistan government, "banned" eleven organisations associated with the proscribed groups JeM/JuD/FIF, under the Natural Action Plan. However, these actions were only cosmetic, and lacked seriousness. They were merely aimed at avoiding blacklisting. For the activities of the JeM, including their operations in J&K and Afghanistan, continued as usual. Activities at JeM's Markaz Usman-o-Ali and Markaz Subhan Allah in Bahawalpur, have resumed. The activities of JeM at Markaz Sunan Bin Salma in Peshawar, Markaz Syedna Bilal in Muzaffarabad (PoJK), Markaz Guru Shaheed in Quetta and other places, also continue as before. The regular movement of trained cadres to and from Afghanistan, has also been noticed.

JeM had vacated their training camps, facilities and detachments in PoJK after Balakot, and shifted cadres to undisclosed locations. Some were asked to return to their homes, while others were accommodated at rented locations. Some of the vacated facilities were manned with minimum capacity for some time. However, after the takeover of the Taliban in Afghanistan, activities of the JeM in PoJK, and the concentration of their cadres at forward camps have been witnessed, indicating a renewed thrust of JeM to infiltrate trained cadres into J&K. A spurt in the activities of JeM at Markaz Syedna Bilal, Panjgaran, Shawai Road, Muzaffarabad, PoJK has come to notice. This markaz acts as a transit camp for JeM cadres, and they report at this markaz prior to infiltration into J&K. Mufti Asghar Khan Kashmiri, Amir, JeM PoJK, who is in-charge of operations in J&K, heads this markaz.

Ibrahim Azhar, the elder brother of Masood Azhar, is currently overseeing JeM affairs in Afghanistan. He was earlier stationed in Muzaffarabad (PoJK) along with Mufti Rauf Asghar Kashmiri, Amir JeM, PoJK since December 2018. They had planned to infiltrate into J&K (May–June 2019) to avenge the killing of Ibrahim's sons, Usman and Umar. He subsequently moved to Leepa Valley (PoJK)/Shakargarh (Punjab, Pakistan) for infiltration, after which he returned to Bahawalpur on Eid. Significantly, a number of JeM high-value operatives, including Afghan war veterans, have been pushed into J&K to intensify terrorist activities. Further, there were attempts to push more senior JeM operatives for intensifying terrorist activities. Senior commanders of JeM like Mufti Abdul Rauf Asghar, de facto Amir, and Maulana Ammar, are engaged in mobilising cadres/logistics, and are holding regular meetings with their ISI handlers regarding training and infiltration of their cadres.

A substantial quantity of arms and ammunition were seized (1–4 June 2021) by the Indian Security Forces (ISFs), which was sent from Pakistan-based JeM handlers via drones from across the border, in the Samba area of the Jammu region. The consignment comprised AK-47 Rifle (2 nos.), AK-47 magazine (8 nos.), pistol (9 mm,10 nos.), pistol magazine (18 nos.), grenades (9 nos.) and pistol rounds (180 nos.). JeM operatives have been responsible for a series of infiltrations and drone-dropping activities to carry out IED attacks on ISF in J&K. Besides, footprints of JeM operatives are found in the outskirts of Srinagar, especially in the Budgam district and the Tral areas of Pulwama district in J&K. A network of JeM cadres, including foreign terrorists, is operating in J&K.

JeM Commanders Abdul Rashid Ghazi and Muhammad Ismail were killed in an encounter with the ISFs on 31 July 2021. Ismail was the key wanted person in the Pulwama attack that took place on 14 February 2019, and he was instrumental in motivating and training Adil Ahmed Dar, who carried out the VBIED suicide attack. He was involved in imparting IED training to local JeM cadres as well. His main handlers were Yousuf Azhar, brother of Maulana Masood Azhar and head of the Balakot training centre, and Mufti Abdul Rauf Asghar. According to reports, from January to November 2021, a total of 149 terrorists including 23 Pakistan-based terrorists, have been neutralised in J&K. Launching hubs across the LoC/IB in PoJK are intact, with an increase in the concentration of terrorists and the attempts at infiltration. Since the abrogation of Article 370, the Pakistani establishment has made concentrated efforts for bulk infiltration of terror cadres into J&K. This was reflected as a considerable shift in infiltration bids via the IB sector (Jammu Zone) from the LoC (Kashmir Valley) and was noticed in the recent past. Besides, Pakistan's ISI is trying every possible means to activate terrorists/OGWs in the Jammu Zone for assisting infiltration.

Many years ago, in Srinagar, I had a long conversation with Firdous Syed, one of those who joined militancy at its very beginning, and then bitterly regretted it. This is an excerpt from that interview:

'We should have the courage to apologise,' argues Firdous Syed. 'The courage to apologise, to say we were wrong, all of us, and to start over, from a Truth and Reconciliation Commission that somehow attempts to turn the page and move on.' Syed has blue eyes and light hair, and never smiles. He was one of the early militants, one of those boys in high school or college who dreamed of revolution, of freedom for "occupied" Kashmir from the Indian government, and took up the rifle to get it. 'We were young, we wanted justice and freedom. We were ready, Pakistan was ready to give us guns. That's how it all started, that's how it was supposed to go on. I got out when, after a few years, I realized that I was fighting against my own people. Women, old people and children started dying, when militants started arriving in larger numbers from across the border, and my, our political battle turned into something else. Into a religious conflict, into a covered war between states, at the expense of which, we, all of us, were the losers. The people of Kashmir, whether Muslim or Hindu.'

Living in a small villa on the outskirts of Srinagar, Syed, who now works as a journalist, barely sums up the years of armed struggle, and after that, the years of loneliness. Those in which he was considered a traitor even by his own family, the years of voluntary imprisonment, of distrust. 'One should have the courage to take responsibility,' he resumes, 'Everyone. Myself, and those like me, for leading our people into a dead-end tunnel, into a war that left forty thousand dead on the ground, and then doing nothing to address the violence, the injustices, the pain of those who were protagonists or witnesses of these years. The Indian government for behaving absolutely unjustly from 1947 to the present, President Musharraf for exporting militants and violence, and playing with the lives of Kashmiris. Shabir Shah, Yaseen Malik and the other political-revolutionary leaders for using the strategy of violence as a means of political struggle, and finally, the local authorities for allowing a military occupation worse than and disproportionate to the magnitude of the problem.'

Only from here, according to Syed, could a new beginning be made.

LINKS WITH TALIBAN

Prior to the US withdrawal from Afghanistan, JeM had stepped up its operations in Afghanistan, fighting along with the Afghan Taliban (Pashtun), in reconnaissance of targets and in attacks against the US/NATO establishments, on the directions of the local leadership of the Afghan Taliban. Of late, the JeM leadership has increased their activities in Afghanistan from Peshawar, KPK. JeM is very active in various mosques of Peshawar, which house Afghan refugees. Jaish has set up another front in Quetta, which is often utilised for Afghanistan operations, particularly in Ghazni (Afghanistan) via Chaman. It has established two bases in Afghanistan, in Kandahar (between Spin Buldak and Kandahar city), and in the northern part of Helmand province. JeM utilises routes via Peshawar, Dera Ismail Khan and Quetta/Baluchistan, for operations in Afghanistan in Kabul/Nangarhar, Khost and Kandahar/Helmand/Ghazni provinces of Afghanistan. JeM currently has cadres active in Nuristan, Kunar, Laghman, Khost, Ghazni, Geelan, Helmand and Nangarhar areas of Afghanistan.

The ties between Taliban and JeM are mainly based on JeM's capability to provide a continuous flow of Pakistani recruits from provinces of South Punjab, Khyber Pakhtunkhwa and tribal/ex-FATA region bordering Afghanistan. A significant number of battle-hardened fighters who have aided the ground successes of Taliban, have their origins in the training camps operated by JeM, which straddle across Punjab and Khyber Pakhtunkhwa. JeM's credibility has also grown from the effectiveness of its suicide bombers, who are often handed over to the Taliban/Haqqani Network for executing attacks in Afghanistan. As per the current modus operandi, the group is assisting the Taliban establishments on the directions of the local leadership. Moreover, with the approval of the local Afghan Taliban leadership, the JeM has also been executing operations inside Afghanistan independently.

JeM's capability related to spectacular suicide attacks and fidayeen operations, has become a major operational component of HQN/Afghan Taliban. While JeM is operating in Afghanistan alongside the Taliban and HQN, it resorts to launching high-value targets, including battle-hardened operatives in Afghanistan, and those belonging to the family members of Maulana Masood Azhar. This helps them in intensifying training, radicalisation and motivation, thereby intensifying recruitment and fund-collection activities in Pakistan.

In the past JeM, through its ISI handlers, has maintained close ties with the Afghan Taliban, and has been providing them with a continuous stream of Pakistani recruits from the provinces of South Punjab, Khyber Pakhtunkhwa and FATA. The JeM's training camps, including the one at Balakot, have supplied a sizeable number of battle-hardened fighters who have aided the ground successes of the Afghan Taliban. Further, the JeM has also provided suicide bombers to the Taliban and the Haqqani Network for executing attacks in Afghanistan. Now, according to local sources, the province of Nangarhar in Afghanistan has practically been handed over by the Taliban, to JeM.

There are a number of training camps in Nangarhar. Some are under the direct control of the Taliban, and they accommodate only small groups of JeM members. Other camps called Mustaquir camps, are used exclusively by JeM. The so-called Khogyani camps are located in the vicinity of the civilian population and have classrooms, grounds and hostels for trainees, residences for instructors, masjids and other facilities. Dargah camps are divided into two parts—accommodation/facilities for in-charges/cadres, masjid, etc. The second portion has accommodation for senior functionaries in the civilian area. According to local sources, earlier, these camps were used for imparting training to Haqqani and Taliban cadres. They have been later handed over to JeM members in lieu of the training facilities provided by JeM to Haqqani fighters in Pakistan. JeM cadres have been shifted to Nangarhar, on ISI's instructions, from the Khyber Agency and from Pan Chinar, on the Pakistan-Afghan border. Since then, new recruits and fresh trainees are brought on a regular basis to these camps, from various districts of Afghanistan and Pakistan. The expenditure of these camps, including maintenance, logistics and salary for instructors, are borne by the JeM.

A number of training camps are located in the Khogyani district of Nangarhar. The camps are located in the proximity of villages or anywhere where civilians live. They have all kinds of facilities, like hostels for trainees, grounds, masjids, classrooms and residences for instructors. In-charges and cadres of JeM are accommodated in separate camps, and share their living spaces with senior functionaries in the civilian areas. The training schedule in the camps includes physical training, classroom lessons, dismantling and assembling of weapons, handling of arms and ammunition, and specialised modules for fidayeen (suicide) attacks. The firing practice is, however, done away from the camp due to the close proximity to civilian locations. Eyewitnesses have seen a range of AK-47, LMG, rocket launchers, grenades, explosives and so much more, being used for training.

The trainees are also given jungle survival training in the Kunar jungle near the Nuristan border. JeM cadres trained at camps in Nangarhar, are being regularly infiltrated into J&K for terrorist operations. The attack on the Sunjuwan Army camp in Jammu in February 2018, was conducted by three Pakistani cadres trained at the Khogyani camp. A number of these trained cadres are active in J&K. There's in fact a specific training schedule for fidayeens deployed in Kashmir. Beside the "ordinary" teachings imparted, the trainees are also given a ten-day special capsule module, which includes storming into army camps, camouflage, concealment, survival techniques and fabrication of IEDs. In addition, 20 days of firing practice and infiltration techniques into replicas of areas like Neelam, Sharda, Kotli, etc., are carried out. The day's schedule is more or less like this:

- *Warjis* or workout, starting early morning, which includes a 45-minute run, dips, and other exercises for weight loss (it appears that even jihadis have weight problems!) and general fitness
- Namaz, because you have to pray
- *Mamulat* or what is a daily spiritual routine
- Then again, *Warjis Asleek* (till 12 pm), training focussed on weapons
- Rest, namaz and lunch
- *Arsah* and *Magreeb* prayers
- Dinner and again *Isha*, the Islamic night prayer
- Again, *Warjis* at night

After completion of this advanced *Tasisiya* training, the group is given a ten-day specialised training, which practically encompasses an even heavier-than-normal brainwashing, and thereafter, the members are infiltrated into J&K. Training also includes the handling of various communication equipment. They are taught to handle wireless or V8 equipment and communication equipment said to be indigenously developed by JeM's engineers in Pakistan. This equipment consists of a wireless set and an LG mobile handset, wherein their motherboards are tuned at the same frequencies. It has the facility to send both voice and text messages. Once a message is sent, it shows one tick, and a read message shows two-ticks. It also has a display of signal strength (1 to 5) and has a good coverage in PoJK. These special handsets are mainly used during infiltration into J&K, and movement near LoC. The communication is facilitated through towers erected at Muzaffarabad (main tower) and other places along the LoC, which are designed for fidayeens who are later deployed in J&K and Afghanistan.

JeM also organises a ten-day refresher course for its senior functionaries on Askari training from time to time. Senior functionaries have to undergo this training at least once a year.

JeM's activities are overseen by key members of Masood Azhar's family as described earlier. Ibrahim Azhar is in charge of the Afghanistan operations, while Mufti Abdul Rauf Asghar and Maulana Ammar also have specific roles. Mufti Abdul Rauf Asghar Kashmiri, is in charge of the Nangarhar camps. This was the same person who supervised the Balakot camp, and who has been in charge of actively recruiting fidayeen cadres for the past few years at least. Asghar, despite being at a point placed officially under protective custody, has been seen holding multiple meetings with ISI operatives at various times.

The same sources maintain that there were a few differences on the issue of jihad between JeM and ISI as narrated earlier. ISI gave very clear directions to Asghar and his associates—they should have supported the Taliban during the first months, focussing on Afghanistan more than on Kashmir. However, Asghar insisted that the group could easily do both, focusing on Kashmir as well as supporting the Taliban. The ISI line, of course, prevailed and JeM, along with LeT, was put on the job of raising funds for the Taliban, and to facilitate the movements of jihadis (including Al Qaida members) from Pakistan to Afghanistan.

The rest is history. Taliban took Afghanistan, and a few days after Kabul's fall, Masood Azhar rushed to Kandahar to meet with Taliban leaders, in order to coordinate joint operations between the two groups. During the meeting, Azhar strongly advocated the need for the two groups to focus on the jihad in Kashmir, instead of pursuing political objectives. So, it is just a matter of time that further activities happen.

In May 2022, the 13th report of the Analytical Support and Sanctions Monitoring Team cited a UN Member State as saying that Jaish-e-Mohammed (JeM) maintains eight training camps in Nangarhar, three of which are directly under Taliban control. It was the first report since the 15 August 2021 takeover of Kabul by the Taliban. It noted that the period between then and April 2022, has seen the Taliban consolidate control over Afghanistan, appointing 41 United Nations-sanctioned individuals to the Cabinet, and other senior-level positions in their de facto administration. They have favoured loyalty and seniority over competence, and their decision-making has been opaque and inconsistent. The report further states that the Tehrik-e Taliban Pakistan (TTP) constitutes the largest component of foreign fighters in Afghanistan, and their number is estimated to run into several thousand. Other groups include the Eastern Turkistan Islamic Movement (ETIM), Islamic Movement of Uzbekistan, Jaish-e-Mohammed, Jamaat Ansarullah and the LeT, each numbering a few hundreds. It also stated that Jaish-e-Mohammed is ideologically and materially closer to the Taliban. It further stated that Qari Ramazan is the newly-appointed head of JeM in Afghanistan. It noted that Lashkar-e-Toiba was described in the previous Monitoring Team reports as having provided finance and training expertise to Taliban operations.

According to the same report, in January 2022, a Taliban delegation visited a training camp used by LeT in the Haska Mena district of Nangarhar. The group was said to maintain three camps in Kunar and Nangarhar. Previous LeT members have included Aslam Farooqi and Ejaz Ahmad Ahangar (aka Abu Usman al-Kashmiri), both of whom joined ISIL-K, the report added. The Haqqani Network is still regarded as having the closest links to Al Qaida. The group continues to be the trusted partner for local facilitation of safe havens and support for the Al Qaida core, including the maintaining of ties with the so-called legacy Al Qaida—those who had long ago established relations with the late Jalaluddin Haqqani and to whom the Haqqanis feel indebted to for supporting them and the Taliban, the report said. The report noted that following the Taliban takeover of Afghanistan in August 2021, the Haqqani Network moved quickly to secure the control of certain key portfolios and ministries—interior, intelligence, passports and migration.

Prominent de facto ministerial positions secured by the Haqqani Network include those occupied by de facto Interior Minister Sirajuddin Haqqani, and de facto Minister for Refugees, Khalil Ahmed Haqqani, it said. Responsibilities associated with these roles appear carefully chosen, as the ministries encompass the issuing of identity cards, passports and the monitoring of persons entering and exiting the country. The Haqqani Network has also become the best militarily-equipped faction, and controls a number of armed formations, including the elite Badri 313 Battalion. The Haqqani Network now largely controls security in Afghanistan, including the security of the capital Kabul, the report noted. The eleventh report of the Analytical Support and Sanctions Monitoring Team had stated that among those groups posing a security threat, Afghan officials highlighted Tehrik-e Taliban Pakistan, Jaish-e-Mohammed and Lashkar-e-Toiba, groups about which the Monitoring Team has written in the previous reports as well. The eleventh report added that according to Afghan interlocutors, Jaish-e-Mohammed and Lashkar-e-Toiba facilitated the trafficking of militant fighters into Afghanistan, who act as advisers, trainers and specialists in improvised explosive devices. Both groups were responsible for carrying out targeted assassinations against government officials and others.

Lashkar-e-Toiba and Jaish-e-Mohammed were stated to have approximately 800 and 200 armed fighters respectively, co-located with Taliban forces in Mohmand Darah, Dur Baba and Sherzad districts of the Nangarhar Province, the report said. In Kunar Province, Lashkar-e-Toiba retains a further 220 fighters, and Jaish-e-Mohammed has a further 30, all of whom are dispersed within Taliban forces, it added. The major attacks which include one on a Guest House in Kabul in May 2015, a January 2016 attack on the Indian Consulate in Mazar-e-Sharif in the Balkh province, an attack on the Indian Consulate in Jalalabad, on the diplomatic area in Kabul and the Ghazni attack, which are listed and described in Chapter 4, make context here again. These attacks are also corroborated by the below:

- The fifteenth report, submitted on 8 July 2024 under Security Council document S/2024/499
- The Analytical Support and Sanctions Monitoring Team also confirms what has been stated in the previous reports
- JeM, along with other terrorist groups, continues to operate within Afghan territory collaborating with other terrorist organisations, including Al Qaida and the Tehrik-e Taliban Pakistan (TTP) and sharing with them resources and training facilities

The link between JeM and Taliban is very strong. To go back to Balakot, according to experts, there was enhanced co-operation between JeM and Afghan Taliban/Haqqani Network (HQN) following the Indian air strike. Since then, the JeM has been relying more and more on its Afghanistan-based cadres. After the Balakot Air Strike, a number of hard-core cadres, particularly belonging to JeM and LeT, were expecting more retaliatory action by Indian forces, and were moved to the Afghanistan-Pakistan border areas. A number of these cadres further infiltrated into Afghanistan, and were accommodated by the Taliban/Haqqani Network (HQN). They have been relocated in coordination with the Taliban in areas including Kot and Momandara (Nangarhar), Sangin and Marja (Helmand), Logar, Nawa (Ghazni), Zurmat (Paktia), Kunar, Faryab and Kunduz.

The coordination between JeM and Taliban/HQN extends to terrorist operations in J&K as well. HQN, as part of its Kashmir operations, is believed to have established centres in PoJK in early January 2019. These centres would be utilised for carrying out guerilla-style and improvised explosive device (IED) attacks against Indian security check posts and installations.

Moreover, the Pakistan government had allotted space to JeM

for training activities beyond Peshawar in the Afghanistan-Pakistan region, wherein JeM had set up a training facility for its cadres at Malakand, KPK. JeM Askari training camps in Pakistan had also been shifted to Afghanistan or to camps along Afghanistan-Pakistan region, while JeM centres in Pakistan are being utilised for religious courses. Earlier, in February 2019, a delegation of Afghan Taliban and HQN commanders held a meeting with the JeM Amir, Maulana Masood Azhar, at Markaz Subhan Allah in Bahawalpur. In view of international pressure, they told Masood Azhar that he should shift his base from Bahawalpur to a secure hideout of the Taliban in Afghanistan. Maulana Masood Azhar, however, assured the Taliban commanders of his continued support from Pakistan itself. Besides, senior JeM functionaries Mufti Abdul Rauf Asghar and Maulana Ammar, had been holding regular meetings with senior Taliban functionaries, including Mullah Mohammad Fazal and Sirajuddin Haqqani, in Afghanistan. The meetings were also attended by ISI officials. Besides, Ibrahim Azhar, who is currently overseeing JeM affairs in Afghanistan, has opened two markaz centres with the Taliban's assistance, at Spin Boldak, Kandahar, and at Jalalabad.

But apparently, Pakistan had only quite recently found out all of this. At one point, according to *Geo News*, the Pakistani government had written an official letter to the Taliban government stating that Masood Azhar was hiding in Afghanistan, living most probably between the provinces of Nangarhar and Kunar. In the letter, apparently, Islamabad was asking the Government of Kabul to arrest the JeM chief and send him back to Pakistan. Nobody has confirmed or denied the news from the Pakistani government, but Bilawal Bhutto, when asked by the press about Masood Azhar, declared, 'Our information is that said individual is in Afghanistan.'

The Taliban reacted almost immediately, stating that, 'The leader of the Jaesh-e-Mohammad group is not here in Afghanistan. This is an organization which could be in Pakistan. Anyway, he is not in Afghanistan and we have not been asked anything like this. We have heard about it in the news. Our reaction is that this is not true.' The spokesperson then added, 'We also call on all parties to refrain from such allegations lacking any proof and documentation. Such media allegations can adversely affect bilateral relations.'

Letter or not, we shall stick to facts. Not so long ago, Pakistan had said that Azhar was under house arrest in Bahawalpur. Then they said they had no idea of his whereabouts. Meanwhile, despite all the claims that he was nowhere to be seen, the JeM chief continued to publish articles on Pakistani social media networks, exhorting JeM cadres to indulge in jihad, praising the Taliban takeover of Kabul, claiming that the Taliban victory would drive Muslim victories elsewhere. It is an open secret that JeM, through its ISI handlers, has maintained close ties with the Afghan Taliban, and has been providing them with a continuous stream of Pakistani recruits from the provinces of South Punjab, Khyber Pakhtunkhwa and FATA.

Al Zawahiri was killed by a drone in Kabul, almost certainly with some level of assistance from Pakistan. And Islamabad, a few months later, got the IMF help it so desperately needed, to have Pakistan removed from the FATF grey list, and grant the billions they poured into the country between 2023 and 2024. This is the reason why not so long ago, the Lashkar-e-Toiba commander Sajjid Mir, declared dead for the longest time, has been abruptly "resurrected" by the Army, and arrested after being declared for years non-existent, unknown, or dead. This is the reason why Mohammed Hafiz Saeed has been "arrested" for the umpteenth time. His arrests almost always coincide with international pressure, such as from the Financial Action Task Force (FATF) or US demands. And this might also be the reason why Masood Azhar had allegedly been shifted to Afghanistan under the protection of the Haqqani. But of course, nobody is so naive as to believe that Islamabad would so easily give up one of its main strategic assets. There's no safer place for Azhar than the place where he's been living and thriving until now, in the loving care of the ISI.

Interestingly enough, China has several times put a hold on a proposal by the US and India at the UNSC, to designate Abdul Rauf Asghar as an international terrorist. Meanwhile, in the most recent and quite an amusing development, the Taliban have been formally accusing Pakistan of providing training camps for ISIS, without openly mentioning ISIS, but by talking of "destabilising projects" or "plots". As usual, the Taliban refers to ISIS and other antagonist groups in a sort of a mirror and smoke strategy. According to the report published in January 2025, a "plot of sedition and destabilisation" has been completely suppressed in Afghanistan. However, some of the leaders of these groups, with indirect support from Pakistan, have begun reorganising themselves. According to the report, '…many commanders, heads of important branches, planners, and executors of major attacks, as well as hundreds of their members (mostly ISIS), have either been killed or arrested.' Meanwhile, '…some of the leaders and members of this group, who fled to neighbouring countries after being suppressed, have once again begun reorganizing with the tolerance, leniency, and indirect support of certain factions.'

The Taliban claims to have credible information that these groups 'are transferring newly recruited forces from several Asian and European countries to their centres in Balochistan and the tribal areas of Khyber Pakhtunkhwa through Karachi and Islamabad airports.' They also claim that 'there is a high likelihood that in the coming months, these individuals may be used to carry out attacks in various countries in the region and globally.'

JIHADI SOCIAL

One of the issues of great global concern is the use of social media by terrorists. There is interplay between home-grown terrorist groups and international terrorist organisations, which plays a central role in accelerating situations. Terrorist organisations use social media platforms for recruiting, training and communicating with their followers, supporters and donors, as it is a cheaper, easier, faster and a more effective method of communication. Members of the terrorist organisations are spreading their ideological thoughts, propaganda and their activities, not only to South Asia but also to the world, using social media platforms. JeM efficiently utilises both offline and online tools for recruitment, and for disseminating their messages. The offline tools include newspapers, magazines, sermons, jihadist songs, publications, posters, banners and relief activities. The offline tools may not be accessible to public at large. However, its effectiveness and outreach increases manifold when many of them are reproduced online.

Al Qalam, and now *Madeena Madeena*, are their main publications. *Al Qalam*, the older of the two, has long been recognised as a flagship publication. It offers a blend of religious commentary, political discourse, and ideological messaging. The latter, the more recent addition to their publication efforts, is issued on a fortnightly basis and appears to target a younger and possibly more diverse audience. It is more vibrant in tone and format, aiming to engage readers through a mix of spiritual writings, cultural commentary, and ideological reinforcement. The magazine has a separate recurring section titled *Rang-o-Noor*, which includes articles of Maulana Masood Azhar, under his pen name Sadi. JeM propaganda material and publications like Muslim Ummah and Sada-e-Mujahid are also distributed regularly across Pakistan. Advertisements for various courses, along with the schedules, are also routinely published in JeM's monthly magazine, *Banat-e-Ayesha*. Besides *Al Qalam*, other weeklies include *Zarb-e Momin* and *Daily Islam*. Most of the content published in these newspapers are based on the glorification of jihad, and the activities of JeM, Taliban, and other militant outfits. The *Al Qalam* newspaper also publishes two monthly magazines, targeting women and children respectively, viz. *Khwateen ka Islam* (targeting women), and *Musalmaan Bache* (for children).

There has also been a remarkable use of social media by JeM (mostly Facebook, WhatsApp and Telegram), to radicalise youth globally, and to rope in Kashmiri youth in particular, for terrorist activities in the Valley. In addition to this, photographs and videos of Gaibana Namaz-e-Janaza (in-absentia funeral prayers) and doctored videos of atrocities by ISF, are continuously posted on social media. JeM's online tools include websites, Facebook Pages/groups, photos/pictures, audio/video, online sermons (Bayanaat), online newspapers/magazines and blogs/forums.

A number of publications are also available online as:
www.rangnoor.com
www.musalmanbchay.com
www.ihueusummat.com
www.alqalamonline.com
www.fathuljawad.com
www.sademujahid.com
www.banateyesha.com
https://t.me//Qafilailmojihad

JeM has actively been involved in spreading anti-India/anti-West and jihadi propaganda in public rallies across Pakistan, as also through print/social media. Jihadi pictures and videos are uploaded regularly by JeM functionaries and cadres, instigating people to devote their life and wealth for jihad. Such sites have members and followers from across nationalities.

According to researchers, 70 per cent of the people of Pakistan have access to mobile phones, whereas only 25 per cent of them have access to conventional media through their mobile phones, Therefore, apart from the other print and electronic media, social media has become an important factor in disseminating information. According to Pakistani intelligence analysts, social media is also a platform for militancy and recruitment. Let me give you a practical example. In August 2022, the online publication *Logically*, carried this very interesting article:

> In an exclusive investigation, Logically has found that Farhatullah Ghauri, a terrorist recruiter and financier for Jaish-e-Mohammed (JeM), a Pakistan-backed terror group, is using a network of accounts on Facebook, Telegram, and YouTube to amplify terrorist propaganda videos targeting religious minorities in the country. JeM is the group responsible for

several terror attacks in India, including the February 2019 Pulwama bombing that led to the death of 40 Indian security personnel. The network was identified by Logically before it could accrue a significant audience peaking with 200-400 subscribers across all the accounts. The terrorist propaganda has circulated across other encrypted messaging channels on Telegram, including those affiliated with Islamabad-backed proxy terror groups claiming to operate in the Kashmir region, such as the Hizbul Mujahideen and The Resistance Front. Closer scrutiny of the amplification patterns of the videos on Facebook since January 2022 suggests a concerted attempt by malicious actors to post the videos in Facebook groups and pages dedicated to socialism, Islam, and minority rights. These groups are frequented by larger, more mainstream audiences of domestic users who are critical of the Bharatiya Janata Party (BJP) government. Moreover, these coordinated online campaigns coincide with offline incidents of communal violence in the country, revealing how malicious actors abroad are leveraging major social media platforms to exploit domestic tensions and radicalise the minority population.

Farhatullah Ghauri is listed among thirty-eight individuals as a terrorist by the Indian Ministry of Home Affairs under the Unlawful Activities (Prevention) Act, 1967 (amended in 2019). Also known as Abu Sufiyan, Ghauri is originally from Kurmaguda district in Hyderabad, India, and is primarily known for being a terrorist financier. He fled to Saudi Arabia in 1994 and finally settled in Pakistan in 2015.

In addition to being a close associate of Masood Azhar, Farhatullah is personally implicated by Indian intelligence services for planning and facilitating a series of terror attacks in the country. These attacks include an improvised explosive device (IED) attack at the Sai Baba Temple in Saroornagar in 2002, a fidayeen (suicide) attack on the Akshardham temple complex in Gujarat the same year, a suicide bomb attack targeting the Hyderabad City Police Commissioner's Task Force office at Begumpet in 2005, and the attempted assassination of Nallu Indrasena Reddy, an Indian politician, a former national secretary of the BJP, who is currently the Governor of Tripura, in 2017. According to intelligence from Indian agencies, Ghauri facilitates and finances these attacks without actively participating in them. He also actively recruits and indoctrinates individuals, including funding their travel from India to Dubai and Pakistan, for radicalisation and training.

In April 2022, *The Print* reported how the fugitive financier had decided to shed decades of anonymity in favour of amplifying propaganda on social media, by following a more overt approach towards recruitment, centred on personal outreach within close circles, mediated by clerics and family ties. Through this approach, he seeks to recruit Indian Muslims to carry out domestic terror attacks on behalf of several other groups, namely, Al Qaida in the Indian Subcontinent (AQIS) and Lashkar-e-Toiba (LeT), symbolic of a broader effort by jihadist groups to leverage popular digital communication platforms to appeal to a new generation of "jihad volunteers", by exploiting domestic communal tensions.

Praveen Swami wrote in August 2019:

Even as the United States has hailed Pakistan for "initial steps" taken against the Jaish-e-Mohammed, the internationally-proscribed terrorist group has remerged on social media platforms—issuing its first public message since Islamabad clamped down on the group in April, amid international pressure. "There are people who are silent, but doing a great deal," reads the Urdu-language message, written over an image of Jaish terrorists in combat uniform, and attributed to the organization's chief, Masood Azhar Alvi. Earlier this week, a United States government official had praised Pakistan in an interview to Geo Television, lauding the steps the country had "taken against Jaish-e-Mohammed and Lashkar-e-Taiba". Indian intelligence officials said the reemergence of the Jaish in the public sphere implied that restraints imposed on it by Pakistan's military were being eased, in response to the unfolding crisis in Jammu and Kashmir. Last week, jihadist social media feeds in Pakistan had also circulated a message attributed to Masood Azhar. "Kashmiris need to get out [on to the streets]", it read. "Then the enemy will beg for peace and negotiation." However, the message, unlike the one released today, did not bear the insignia of the Jaish-e-Mohammed, or its official publication, al-Qalam. The Jaish-e-Mohammed's message appeared targeted towards Islamists in Kashmir, among whom the Inter-Services Intelligence-backed group has long been seeking to expand its reach. In Srinagar's Soura area, where Islamist-led youth who have barricaded streets with trees and barbed wire, protestors have flown the flag of the Jaish-e-Mohammed on multiple occasions. The protestors have also attacked Central and state police forces who have been seeking to seal the grounds around the Jinaab Sahib shrine. Home to large numbers of migrants from Srinagar's congested old city neighbourhoods, the traditional bastions of the city's religious right-wing, Soura is among the strongholds of the secessionist movement in Kashmir—notably registering zero voter turnout in local body elections last year. Police also came under attack by stone-throwing mobs on Wednesday, when they cordoned off Baramulla's Gani Hamam neighbourhood for a counter-terrorism operation—the first since Article 370 was abrogated by Parliament. The operation led to the killing of Lashkar-e-Taiba jihadist Ghulam Rasool Gojri, who was reported to have left his home in the city and joined the terrorist group at the end of July. Faced with the sanctions from the multinational Financial Action Task Force, Islamabad says it has brought seminaries linked to jihadist groups under government administration and is prosecuting key leaders for financing terrorism. But Lahore-based sources said that weapon-wielding Lashkar-e-Taiba personnel were still visible around the organization's headquarters at Lahore's Chowburji. Public entry to the Jaish-e-Mohammed's seminaries in Bahawalpur, the sources said, also remained blocked by guards belonging to the organization. Last month, a United Nations watchdog raised fears cadre of these jihadist groups were also training with the Taliban in Afghanistan, who it said "cooperate and retain strong links with Al Qaeda, in the Indian Subcontinent, the Haqqani Network, [and] the Lashkar-e-Taiba". Prominent Pakistani clerics have called for jihad against India at rallies over the last week. Mufti Abdul Qavi—a member of the ruling Tehreek-e-Insaaf Party, who gained notoriety when he was filmed attempting to seduce slain social-media star Qandeel Baloch—said last week that it was "moral and shari'a-based obligation on Muslims living in India that they support the oppressed Kashmiri Muslims in their jihad".

The importance of social media for jihad can be better understood, taking into consideration what happened with the Taliban. As Kabul fell to the Taliban in mid-August 2021, a rallying cry inundated social media platforms globally. The digital drumbeat could be heard across Facebook posts, Instagram comment threads, and Telegram channels. It was amplified by digital characters now ubiquitous in online meme culture, such as Pepe the Frog, Wojak, and GigaChad. Those posting the memes were not just members of the so-called alt-right, though they too united around the call, but also young jihadists, who are piecing together a new online aesthetic inspired by the world's most notorious internet trolls.

In the early days of the Taliban takeover of Kabul, images emerged on platforms like Twitter (now X), depicting what appeared to be Taliban-sponsored "journalists"—young boys holding microphones, interviewing local peers who expressed enthusiasm for Mullah Baradar and his promises of a renewed era of "peace and prosperity". The scenes struck many observers as surreal, even strangely enchanting, offering a carefully curated portrayal of normalcy and optimism under the new regime. To the unwary, these vignettes seemed to legitimise the Taliban's narrative of change.

The images were posted on Twitter by Zabihullah Mujahid, the official spokesman for the new rulers, who finally, amidst endless articles in the Western and non-Western press, unveiled his face after years to make a splash in the media, appearing on every possible national and international network in a tightly orchestrated media blitz. Mujahid, as well as the other spokesman Suhail Shaheen, engaged with virtually every major media outlet from 15 August onwards, repeating a well-rehearsed message of "peace and prosperity" under the new Taliban rule. This new digital-savvy Taliban harnessed the convergence of memes, disinformation, and mainstream media appearances, to recast its image. In doing so, it revealed a sophisticated understanding of modern information warfare—one that blends radical ideology with the memetic logic of the internet. A deliberately diverse and ostensibly inclusive leadership council was assembled, designed to project an image of a reformed movement—far removed from the brutal regime that had once ruled Afghanistan, and that had infamously, mutilated and killed former President Mohammad Najibullah, stuffing his genitals into his mouth before hanging his body in public. In short, we could call it the "give peace a chance" party (candles in hand and closed-mouth choruses can be imagined as optional), virtually headed by Zalmay Khalilzad, the US special envoy to Doha, the architect of the infamous mess pompously dubbed "peace accords".

The gospel according to Khalilzad, passed along to various official US and non-US authorities at that time, was instrumental in constructing the surreal notion of this "new Taliban", to be more in accordance with the times, as Taliban 2.0. The narrative began by praising the open-mindedness of those who until the other day, had been cheerfully slitting the throats of civilians and military personnel while negotiating the surrender of the United States. Under this emerging consensus, the Taliban were reinvented: not as brutal jihadists, but as pragmatic nationalists ready to govern responsibly. They solemnly promised that girls would soon return to school, and women would be able to resume work—"as soon as the security situation allowed".

The old Taliban, incidentally, used to say the same thing. The emergency preventing their women from leaving the house lasted throughout their rule, from 1996 to 2001. But then again, who remembered that anymore? The new Taliban promised a general amnesty for collaborators and traitors (read: officials, military and policemen serving under the American-created regime). Then, they hunted down and murdered in cold blood anyone who had anything to do with the "occupation forces". But since they did this without cameras around, no one bothered to officially refute their lies. The new Taliban, moreover, had solemnly promised to sever their ties with Al Qaida and other assorted jihadis, and not to allow Afghanistan to be used as a preferred hub for terrorists of all kinds.

It was another matter that in the aftermath of the taking of Kabul, Masood Azhar, a UN-designated terrorist, was in Kandahar along with other bigwigs of the organisation to meet with Baradar and comrades. Amin-ul-Haq, one of Osama bin Laden's closest associates, returned with full honour to his native Nangarhar. To top it all, heading the security of the "new" Taliban was Sirajuddin Haqqani, head of the Haqqani Network, which was still on the UN list of terrorist organisations and proficient in suicide bombings. For example the one at Kabul airport, claimed by Islamic State-Khorasan Province (ISIS-K), bore the Haqqani's fingerprints everywhere. And yet, these were the Taliban 2.0, "separate entities", according to Washington, from the Haqqanis. The Taliban must be given a chance. The Haqqanis, and especially ISIS-K, have nothing to do with former theology students.

The fact that ISIS-K enjoys very close ties with both the Taliban and the Haqqani Network, and that Haqqani and Taliban have been working together for 20 years, means nothing. Just as it means nothing that Pakistan, where all these gentlemen have been staying for the past two decades, remotely managed the above organisations by having them play on the same team or against each other according to convenience. Repeating the old story of good terrorists and bad terrorists—the Taliban 2.0 are good and want peace, ISIS-K is bad. Support must be given to the Taliban, and more importantly, the purse strings must be reopened if ISIS-K is to be defeated. The strategy has paid off for years, and it continues to pay off. Not the least because it is now supported by an image campaign in a big way.

The Taliban are new, in fact, at least in one respect: social presence and media strategy. 'Today's Taliban are extremely capable and experienced in using the press and social media. Nothing like the Taliban of 20 years ago,' commented Rita Katz, executive director of the SITE Intelligence Group. The advance towards Kabul, was in fact preceded and followed by an unprecedented media offensive. This was so well-managed and so sophisticated, it left many observers wondering whether the Taliban had hired a public relations agency of some sort. Many also wondered who had given them a hand in setting up such a sophisticated propaganda machine.

While no definitive answer emerged, many analysts noted striking similarities between the Taliban's social media strategy and the digital operations once employed by the Islamic State. This comparison was all the more remarkable given the Taliban's historically limited media engagement—a group that, not long ago, had trouble even getting members to pose for ID cards. At least in theory, because the real relationship between the fighters and the camera had already been pointed out in 2003, by Thomas Dworzak, a Magnum photographer, who had collected in a delightful booklet titled *Taliban*, the photos of the aforementioned fighters, the ones taken for their families: a compilation of portraits taken in local studios across Pakistan and Afghanistan—posed, colourised, sometimes touched up to appear more glamorous, in which the fighters appear with kajal in their eyes, lip gloss and glitter sandals, surrounded by flowers and with Kalashnikovs in-hand.

The Taliban's media parable began before that of the Islamic State, followed very closely by the social presence of other groups that have greater links with the Taliban—the Lashkar-e-Toiba and the Jaish-e-Mohammed. It is no coincidence that Masood Azhar was spotted in Kandahar. The relationship between the two groups is very close—the JeM supplies suicide bombers to the Haqqani, to whom the Taliban first contracted the management of suicide attacks. The Taliban then gave them the security management of the new government in Kabul. The two groups have joint training camps, both in Afghanistan and Pakistan. This connection is far from incidental. Many among the senior ranks of the so-called "Taliban 2.0"—the more polished, internationally presentable leadership—lived, studied, and were trained in Pakistan over the past two decades. Their familiarity with digital tools, messaging techniques, and even basic PR strategy, owes more to Pakistani institutions and environments than to any organic evolution from within Afghanistan. When evaluating the Taliban's new media savviness then, it's often unnecessary to search too far for explanations—a glance just across the Durand Line will suffice.

According to research conducted by Alto Analytics, the Taliban have demonstrated an impressive ability to distribute and generate social content to spread their word. They managed to generate about 1,700 tweets in less than two hours—which means, again according to Alto Analytics, publishing in that time, eight videos, an average of four pieces of written content, and about fifty press releases. In addition, according to a survey published by the *The New York Times*, more than one hundred new Twitter and Facebook accounts were created just before they took power again, accounts linked to the Taliban or of open supporters of the said Taliban. These are in addition to the several accounts already in the hands of high-ups in the local jihad elite, both Pakistani and Afghani. This veritable network of real and more often fake social accounts, worked in concert to post videos, slogans, various images and press releases. The

Taliban's messages—like clockwork—were reposted, shared, and retweeted across a carefully cultivated network of accounts. The goal was simple: volume becomes legitimacy. As each tweet echoed the last, the message eventually reached users and platforms far removed from the Taliban's ideological orbit.

At that moment, the news is coated with a more or less a labile varnish of truth, because it comes from a "conventional" source. Does this sound familiar? To those who deal with jihadi organisations, including state organisations in the geopolitical area, it certainly does. It is therefore, worthwhile as always, when it comes to the Taliban and other assorted jihadis, to take a look around Islamabad, just to be on the safe side.

In the beginning was, again, the ever-regretful Director of Inter-Service Public Relations, the legendary Lieutenant General Asif Ghafoor. For a couple of years, Ghafoor was a media star of the first magnitude on Twitter (now X) until once, when drunk in the middle of the night, he started tweeting outrageous things even for an undisputed troll prince. Fired and sent to quell peasant uprisings in southern Punjab, he left an unbridgeable void among Twitter users, and the company that produces Burnol (a local ointment against various burns, whose use Our Lord called for quite often) without its most valuable informal testimonial. A more sober general was promoted in his place, and the Islamabad-made troll factory invented by Ghafoor, modelled on those in China or Russia, has been keeping a lower profile ever since. Which does not mean, however, that it is not still in business. On the contrary, it has become even more efficient because it works out of the spotlight. In fact, for many years, ISPR has been hiring boys and girls in a steady stream. Ads appear in newspapers and TV, and company photos posted (also in Ghafoor's time) here and there, show legions of young people busy running fake social media accounts. On X, it is not even that difficult to recognise them. What they all have in common, is that they are followed by a certain gentleman, a self-proclaimed "journalist" whom no one has ever heard of. They follow each other, and regularly insult anyone who posts content contrary to the general command's directives.

Back to the ISPR's golden age handling of social media, trolls were not and are not the only weapon employed. Ghafoor had created a team of six or seven so-called Western female bloggers/travellers who were paid to tour Pakistan (under escort) propagating the country's beauty, the kindness of its inhabitants, and the respect shown by Pakistani males toward female solo travellers. One such tweet by a Katherine George, went viral at a point, because she praised the kindness and courtesy of Pakistani men in the context of a particularly gruesome rape case that had happened just days before. The account showed the profile photo of a white, blonde girl claiming to be a "sportswoman, tourist, eReader addict, and blogger". It took the X and Instagram crowds a few minutes, however, to discover that the photos posted by "traveller" Katherine were actually of a Polish girl working in Pakistan with a travel agency, and that Katherine George does not exist at all.

Yet another leftover of the past Ghafoor teams? Not quite. Because, scrolling through her timeline, it took little to realise that Katherine's first name was probably Zhao or Li. One of her first tweets, which had 11.9K interactions in just a few minutes, was in fact, "#YearOfTheOx Happy Chinese New Year! May this Year of the Ox bring you a prosperous and healthy 2021. Kiong Hee Huat Tsai! #China". A coincidence? Certainly not. Three-quarters of the alleged Ms George's tweets were in fact about Gwadar and Balochistan, and featured in the vast majority of retweets from another account called Gwadar Pro. Gwadar

Pro is an app, available for both Google and Apple, launched in March 2019 during the "Gwadar Expo", for the purpose of "connecting Gwadar to the rest of the world". The app offers a number of useful tools: an English-Chinese-Urdu translator, an airline ticket service, hotel reservations, and exchange rates. But most importantly, it offers a news service, in which you can find pearls of Chinese and Pakistani propaganda. The app is managed and developed by China Economic Net, and it also has X and Instagram accounts. Gwadar Pro, China Economic Net, and Xinhua Service, which completes the picture, are all primarily focused on Gwadar and the China-Pakistan Economic Corridor. They constantly mention each other's relationships by amplifying their social media presence through a network of fake accounts. The same accounts, Chinese with Pakistani names or vice versa, constantly amplify the friendship between the two peoples. In fact, it is no coincidence that in Ghafoor's time, Liljian Zhao (whose first name, Mohammad, has long since disappeared from his biographies) was at the Chinese Embassy in Islamabad, and later promoted to being the Chinese government spokesman for the ranks he earned in the field. In March 2020, while people in Italy were dying of Covid like flies, the same gentleman launched a shameful Twitter campaign by posting fake videos with the hashtag #thanksChina, in which Italians shouted from balconies to the accompaniment of the Chinese national anthem, to thank their eastern "brothers" for donated aid. Interesting note: the same videos, with a changed national anthem, were posted under the hashtag #thanksPakistan.

According to research compiled by Alchemy Spa's R&D Lab in collaboration with Deweave, Luiss Data Lab and Catchy, more than half of the tweets posted between 11 March and 22 March 2020, with the various hashtags of "thanks China" were generated by bots, automated accounts created for propaganda purposes to serve as a sounding board. The same happened in Pakistan with Liljian Zhao's tweets showing Uyghurs dancing happily in the streets of Xinjiang, and mosques so neatly painted that they looked like stage sets. The same goes for accounts linked to the Taliban, the Jaish-e-Mohammed or the Lashkar-e-Toiba.

For those who think this is fantasy politics or conspiracy theorising, it is worth recalling another episode. The French website of the China Global Television Network launched an interview with Laurene Beaumond, a "freelance journalist based in France". Beaumond, according to the network, is French, took two degrees from the Sorbonne and has "collaborated with all the major French media outlets". Beaumond lived seven years in China, specifically in Urumqi, the capital of Xinjiang. She claims not to recognise at all, in the Xinjiang described by the Western media, where persecution is taking place and real cultural and physical genocide is being carried out, the Xinjiang she experienced. Beaumond accused Western media of mystification, and described her personal Xinjiang as the land of bells and whistles. Does this sound a lot like Liljian Zhao's tweets? This is no accident. Because Laurene Beaumond, as well as Katherine George, do not exist. There is no trace of her in any French newsroom, at the local bar association or on social media.

Madame Beaumond is in fact part of the latest propaganda stunt of the Beijing-Islamabad union—a fake journalist. More precisely, fake female journalists. Better if blonde and Western. Side note: the only other site to have taken up and published in full, the interview with the fake Beaumond was Defence.pk, run by the Pakistani military. The principle is actually very simple—have the same false statement repeated by multiple, disparate, "authoritative" sources, and it automatically becomes an almost-truth.

It is in the same way that the brand "Taliban 2.0" is becoming gospel truth. Which post the Taliban takeover of Afghanistan, is being amplified as already highlighted, not only by bots and fake accounts, but also by respectable and more-than-decent Western and non-Western media. The clearance of the Taliban, especially the Haqqani Network, which, it is worth remembering, is on the list of terrorist groups of all international institutions and many individual states, began with the publication, in *The New York Times* no less, of an editorial by Sirajuddin Haqqani. An "armed and dangerous" terrorist, as the CIA's ban reads, whom the American newspaper chose to give a voice to, by publishing a carefully thought-out article that said all the right things—everything that is liberal and non-liberal America, and echoes what the West wants to hear. Whoever wrote the article, and it certainly was not Haqqani, knew exactly which keys to use. The misguided, and there are quite a few of them, assumed that the Islamabad government's hiring of one of America's leading lobbying firms had paid off.

Haqqani in fact, like the Taliban, has also lived and operated in and from Pakistan for the past twenty years. From his hideout, he moved only to go to his post in Kabul, as security chief of the new government. Who better to control and manage terrorists than another terrorist? Meanwhile, in the media and social media, the "charm offensive" to turn a group of cutthroats into Taliban 2.0, began immediately. The principle is always the same: repeat something and continue to repeat it until it becomes true. Even if the truth of the facts will then disprove it.

The Taliban's social offensive began way back in 2011, according to the Atlantic Council in Washington DC, when former theology students evidently graduated and landed on

Twitter, and then in 2014, created their first Telegram channel. The first videos shot by jihadi operatives began to circulate timidly in the following years, leading up to a full-fledged offensive in 2019. Currently, the Taliban's social media presence is all over the place. They post on X, Telegram and WhatsApp in six languages—Arabic, English, Pashtun, Persian, Turkish and Urdu. Some chats are highly confidential, others less so, but all work in much the same way. And since the messages shared show the participants' phone numbers, one deduces that jihadi sympathisers or wannabes are mostly from Saudi Arabia, Kuwait, Pakistan, the UAE and Afghanistan itself.

Then there is *El-Emarah*, an official channel of the Islamic Emirate of Afghanistan, which functions as a magazine and also as a news agency. *El-Emarah* is broadcast via Telegram, and also has an official website. Since 8 August 2019, *El-Emarah* also appeared on Twitter to share videos and news stories regarding the capture of towns and cities in the advance towards Kabul. At the same time, a few hundred pro-Taliban accounts became active, and shared and retweeted the videos launched by *El-Emarah,* totalling more than half a million views in less than 24 hours. The same videos were later launched by a more official source. A well-known open source intelligence think-tank based in London, has indeed become overnight, one of the biggest supporters of the "new" Taliban, insisting that these poor guys should be given a chance to prove their bonafides to the world. The same think-tank, at the hands of one of its leaders, posted videos of the fighters having fun driving bumper cars, eating ice cream, and riding on swings, with the comment that "after all, these kids never had a childhood".

On the other hand, *CNN's* Clarissa Ward, before she was forced to flee Kabul because she was targeted by the poor boys without a childhood, commented that: '...they scream "death to America", but they look so friendly.' And friendly, Kalashnikovs in hand, second-ranking members of the Taliban comically appeared, looming behind TV anchors during live news broadcasts. The attempt to humanise a gang of predatory cutthroats is apparently succeeding with remarkable ease. So is Islamabad's umpteenth strategic blackmail—recognise the Taliban if you do not want Afghanistan to become a centre of international terrorism once again. "Recognising the Taliban" means in fact, principally, unblocking the Afghan government's foreign accounts. It means giving international legitimacy to the Taliban 2.0, and above all, starting to fund Pakistan again so that it can take in Afghan refugees.

Curiously, among the most ardent print supporters of the new Taliban are the Chinese media, who on social media, backed by the Pakistanis, continue to play the little game that has succeeded so well with Covid or Gwadar and other pieces of the Belt and Road Initiative. One looks forward in some time to the first accounts of ladies praising life under the Taliban some time soon. The great mutation has just begun, but it comes from very far. Osama bin Laden had used publicity from a very young age, revealing himself to be more contemporary than other ideologues. These contemporaries were radicals in their dealings with the media, with the exception of his mentor Abdullah Yusuf Azzam, who was so confident in his communicate on strategy that he financed publications in Arabic to support the Afghan mujahideen against the Soviets in the media.

Osama, with the magazine *al-Jihad*, recruited followers, attracting conspicuous and continuous grants. From a London office, active between 1994 and 1998, the Advice and Reform Committee (ARC), the British office of what later became the Al Qaida, published letters and statements, fostered communication between Qaeda groups, and engaged in unusual self-promotion, so much so that *CNN* and the Arab broadcaster Al Jazeera interviewed Osama in 1997 and 1999 respectively, giving him an undoubted propaganda opportunity not only in the Islamic world, but to the world at large. Thereafter, Osama was no longer interviewed, partly because the setting for the conversations were often Qaeda training camps in Afghanistan, the existence of which the Taliban regime has always denied. Radical groups use the web to disseminate information and messages, and this has resulted in the rise of media groups, producers and distributors of jihadist material for the web, which use a system of online channels operating almost autonomously, with a very marked pervasiveness. The network becomes the substitute for training camps, avoids economic and material expenditures, shortens time, as well as connects with charismatic leaders or followers. The platform aggregates, urges a sense of belonging and proud adherence to the original Islamic cultural heritage, strengthens personal and communal identity, as well as reinvigorates moral values, rules of conduct, dress codes, and lifestyles.

However, unlike their predecessors, the post 9/11 generation of young internet jihadists is no longer simply defined by their ideological affinities. This is a generation that was born into a global war on terror, that came of age during the rise of the Islamic State, and witnessed the Taliban taking back control of Afghanistan. They are Generation Z jihadists, and are for many reasons, increasingly difficult to deal with.

NO WAR, NO PEACE

Many years ago, the Indian philosopher Jiddu Krishnamurti wrote in one of his journals: "Peace is not absence of war". I've read it many years ago, and this quote always came to mind each time I had to describe situations developing in the Indian subcontinent. Absence of war does not necessarily mean peace. And this is exactly how six years later, an Indian Army General describes the current situation with Pakistan: "No War, No Peace."

I have been asking a number of people, if and how Balakot really was the game changer it appeared to be, what lesson could be learned or has been learned from it. I have been asking Indians, and I have also been asking a certain number of Pakistani journalists. However, either declined to reply or claimed to know very little about the topic. Apparently, after the Hamid Mir "crows and trees" show, the Pakistani media maintained the official narrative and immediately shifted coverage to the F16 dispute and the pathetic media show that followed. Pakistani official sources declined to comment, and anyway, it can be noticed how there is a fairly wide literature on Balakot from the Indian side, and almost close to nothing from the Pakistani side.

However, in 2022, the Stimson Center published a series of four essays titled *Regional Roundtable: Reflections on Balakot*, in which:

> Three years after the Pulwama/Balakot crisis, contributors from India, Pakistan, the United States, and China reflect on the escalation that took place, the lessons of the crisis, and the emerging trends to watch in the years ahead. In this series, Lt. Gen. Deependra Singh Hooda (retd.) looks at the ways both India and Pakistan were able to claim victory after the crisis, [and] he notes: "The scale and scope of India's military options against Pakistan in response to major terrorist attacks has indeed widened. However, the fears that this will lead to a swift escalation with the looming danger of a nuclear exchange are overblown." Brig. Imran Hassan meanwhile emphasizes that, "For Pakistan, the lessons from 2019 represent a dangerous move towards limited war below the nuclear threshold." In an interview with the South Asian Voices editorial team Lisa Curtis, Deputy Assistant to the President and NSC Senior Director for South and Central Asia from 2017-2021, reviews the successes and lessons learned from the U.S. response and offers advice for future policymakers. Finally, Zhang Li, Professor of International Relations at the Institute for South Asian Studies at Sichuan University, examines China's role in mediation and perceptions of the crisis.

The first thing you notice while reading the essays is that not once are "crows and trees" quoted, nor is the "precise miss" brought to attention. The focus, and rightly so, is on the lessons learned, in a political and geopolitical sense, from Balakot. As Lt Gen Deependra Singh Hooda (Retd) wrote: 'After the situation had eased, both India and Pakistan claimed victory. This implies that the two countries have learned different lessons from the crisis, which is likely to have implications for how military force is used in the event of a future crisis.'

From an Indian perspective, as it has been highlighted by many sides, the Balakot episode called out Pakistan's nuclear blackmail strategy, and ended years of India's forced restraint in fear of a possible nuclear escalation. Speaking at a seminar in 2020, the Indian Chief of Air Staff, Air Chief Marshal RKS Bhaduria, stated: 'Balakot was a clear demonstration that there exists a space within the sub-conventional conflict boundary wherein the Air Force can be used for targeting and yet have escalation control.' Airstrikes, translating in current language, are way more effective and less risky than sending troops across the LOC as it happened in September 2016, when the Indian Director General of Military Operations announced that the army had "conducted surgical strikes" at terrorist launch hubs across the LoC. Back then, Pakistan stated that a military response was not necessary since the military action never happened.

On Pakistan's part, the PAF's retaliatory strike on 27 February named "Operation Swift Retort" was also claimed as a victory. Pakistan's Air Chief Marshal Mujahid Anwar Khan, said that a "befitting reply" had been given to the "enemy's misadventure" and that "the PAF's swift response was the demonstration of our firm resolve, capacity and capability in thwarting the nefarious designs of the adversary". Former US Secretary of State Mike Pompeo wrote that he spoke with his then Indian counterpart Sushma Swaraj, who told him Pakistan was preparing to launch a nuclear attack against India. 'I do not think the world properly knows just how close the India-Pakistan rivalry came to spilling over into a nuclear conflagration in February 2019. The truth is, I don't know precisely the answer either; I just know it was too close.' Avoiding civilian casualties and in some way allowing both sides to claim victory has been, according to many international analysts, a Solomonic solution to "send a message" while controlling a possible escalation.

Going back to Retd Air Chief Marshal Dhanoa: 'The purpose of the Balakot strike was to tell Jaish-e-Mohammad that if you carry out terrorist attacks on Indian soil, whether you are in Pakistan-occupied Kashmir or you are in Pakistan, we will get you. And, they got the message loud and clear. We had no major terror strike throughout the Indian elections even after Article 370 was revoked in Kashmir and till I retired as the Chief of Air Staff. That was my goal and I achieved it.' Words echoed years later by the Indian External Affairs Minister, S. Jaishankar, 'The calculus of national security has become much more complicated. Traditional methods of competing and pressuring are buttressed by new tools of influence and disruption. Here too, Bharat has pushed back with determination and fortitude.... On the Western front, the long standing challenge of cross-border terrorism now elicits more befitting responses. Believe me, Uri and Balakot sent their own message.'

The extent of the message could be seen five years later in Srinagar, and all over Kashmir. Five years since, on 5 August 2019, in what is widely described as a veritable *coup d'état*, the government in New Delhi had by a quite brilliant technical expedient, swept away Article 370 of the Indian Constitution that enshrined the autonomy of the state of Jammu & Kashmir. It created two Union Territories—Jammu & Kashmir and Ladakh—and wiped out in one fell swoop a conniving and corrupt political class, as well as the "disputed region" status of Kashmir. Simplifying this: if the state of Kashmir no longer exists, neither does the "disputed region", disputed by Pakistan, which it should be remembered, had illegally occupied half of Kashmir and later ceded part of it to China. Pakistan continues to base much of its foreign policy on Kashmir, and remotely continued to pilot for some thirty years, a series of assorted jihadi groups that over time had mutated the region into a veritable war zone. Garrisoned by the Indian Army, subject to curfews so frequent, the state kept schools and stores closed for much of the year.

The prophets of the jihad word had done the rest, opening fundamentalist madrasas financed with Pakistani and Saudi money, closing libraries, cinemas, theatres and art galleries, threatening musicians and actors, throwing paint and sometimes acid at girls who refused to wear the hijab. Cut off from development from the rest of the country and the rest of the world, Kashmir had found itself economically on its knees. The lack of jobs, prospects and distractions had spawned a class of angry young people who clung to backward Islamism and armed struggle not out of conviction, but only to protest against the government and the status quo, without even grasping the contradiction in terms that followed. They invoked the internet, cinemas, theatres and shopping malls, in the name of a verb that denied all these things. Dark years or as we would say in Italy, "years of lead", from which there seemed to be no way out, especially when the abolition of Article 370 was followed by "spontaneous protests" in which, however, instead of Kashmiri flags, ISIS flags were flown. Pakistan then began to invoke freedom for Kashmir, from every international platform. It counted evidently, on the base of local jihadis trained over the years to act as needed and on maintaining the perennial state of war.

Surprisingly, India managed to shift the narrative in Kashmir. Islamabad discovered that no one wants to be free of freedom and a growing economy, and that to put it bluntly, no one makes a revolution if they have a full belly. In fact, five years later, Srinagar appeared transformed. A different world. A world in which the G20 Tourism Ministers' meeting was held in May 2023 without the slightest problem. A world in which stores were open and finally full of customers, of packed hotels with prices now skyrocketing, of house boats booked a year in advance, and shikhara (the local boats) cheerfully carrying around droves of tourists. A world of luxury hotels and restaurants. And this revival was not limited to Srinagar alone, but extended across Kashmir, including towns like Baramulla, which had previously gained attention mainly due to violence and unrest.

Baramulla had a 31-year-old mayor, Shabir Ahmad Khan. A boy who grew up during Kashmir's turbulent "years of lead". Like many in his generation, he expressed frustration with the past conflict and simply wanted a normal life for his community. As mayor, he had championed peace and development, and had fought for it. 'People, ordinary people, have no idea what Article 370 was about. Their main concern, the problem they have, are jobs, government jobs. But this is our internal matter and we'll have to deal with it. Young people want jobs, they want peace. If this move by the government has brought and will bring investment to Kashmir, it is welcome. [I say this] although I don't vote BJP, and I am politically opposed to this government.'

And investment has indeed come. Even from the UAE, which is investing in shopping malls. It is said that Saudi Arabia and Qatar will follow suit. Quite a difference compared to the serial madrasas financed in the past. Meanwhile, the region's traditional exports are flourishing again—apples, cherries, almonds, saffron, lavender and even cricket equipment. Plus the "usual" pashmina shawls, inlaid wood and painted paper mâché artifacts, with an unexpected Cheddar cheese company also making an appearance.

Tourism is bouncing back strongly. Gulmarg's golf courses and ski slopes are once again accessible, and taken by storm. Left to "defend" the human rights of Kashmiris, burdened with hordes of tourists and thriving businesses, are only 'two champions of human rights like Pakistan and China,' and a few sad and melancholy figures in Srinagar, who make a living by taking foreign journalists around and telling them how miserable the lives of Kashmiris are—why it is better to be dead, than to live in prosperity but under "the Indian yoke".

China and Pakistan, on the other hand, cannot abdicate their roles. China because it has been trying for years to push the Belt and Road Initiative across Kashmiri borders. Pakistan because, without the enemy at its doorstep and without Kashmir to "recapture", it loses its *raison d'être*. Or rather, the Army in Islamabad loses its main *raison d'être*. It is no coincidence that every Pakistani premier or president who has ventilated to the contrary on the matter has been taken out, symbolically or materially.

And yet, now, as they used to say, the base, the hard core, is missing. Kashmiri kids are much more interested in becoming influencers on Instagram or playing music in garages than in making revolution. And the shift is palpable. Indian troops on the ground are still there, but people's perceptions have changed. While Indian troops remain stationed across the region, the public's perception of them has evolved. They are no longer seen as outright enemies, but rather as a force preventing attacks—like bombings or the notorious "pilgrim shootings" targeting Hindu visitors to the Amarnath shrine each summer. 'The Indian attack on the Jaish-e-Mohammed training camp in Balakot sent a strong message. The abolition of Article 370, but more importantly, the wave of investment and openness that followed, did the rest,' claims a senior local official, who adds, 'The perception has changed, the atmosphere has changed. Earlier, to commute to my office, I had four established routes that were constantly being changed depending on the day. Now, I take the car and go alone by the shortest route. And if I'm late, they know it was traffic and not a bomb that slowed me down.'

Of course, the guard still remains high. Cross-border infiltrations have not stopped, and sporadic violence continues to erupt. One of the most significant incidents took place in April 2023, just after the then Pakistan's (acting) foreign minister, Bilawal Bhutto Zardari, had put on yet another show in Goa, during a Shanghai Cooperation Organisation meeting—a platform he was given only because he is the son of the late Benazir Bhutto. Bilawal's intervention barely touched any global issue and focused only on advocating for "Kashmir's freedom". And of course, his concern was for Kashmiris in India and not for those in so-called Azad Kashmir, the ones put in jail for blasphemy or forcibly conscripted by the Jaish-e-Mohammed. Almost immediately after his speech, an attack targeted security forces in Poonch. In the end, says a well-known intellectual, 'It all boils down to the familiar clash of cultures. On one side of the border, a mindset that continues to allow people like Lashkar-e-Toiba chief Mohammed Hafiz Saeed to boast that "the Kashmir issue can only be resolved in one way: jihad, jihad, jihad". On the other side, a focus on transforming Kashmir into a hub of tourism, investments and development.'

A concept that Pakistan refuses to acknowledge, in the same way as it refuses to let go of the usual, consolidated strategy of using terrorism as a tool of foreign politics even when the strategy and the tools prove to be more or less deadly, boomeranging against the same State that created it. 'Although "azad" means "free", the residents of Azad Kashmir are anything but,' said Brad Adams, Asia director at Human Rights Watch.

'The Pakistani authorities govern Azad Kashmir with strict controls on basic freedoms.'

This control starts from elections and the electoral process. According to locals and international reports, anyone who wants to take part in public life has to sign a pledge of loyalty to Pakistan, while anyone who publicly supports or works for an independent Kashmir is persecuted. According to a local, the document states: 'No person or political party in Azad Jammu and Kashmir (AJK) shall be permitted to propagate against, or take part in activities prejudicial or detrimental to, the ideology of the State's accession to Pakistan.' Yet another document disqualifies anyone running for elected office who does not sign a declaration that says, 'I solemnly declare that I believe in the Ideology of Pakistan, the Ideology of the State's Accession to Pakistan and the integrity and sovereignty of Pakistan.'

In its report "Update of the Situation of Human Rights in Indian-Administered Kashmir and Pakistan-Administered Kashmir from May 2018 to April 2019", released on 8 July 2019, the United Nations stated:

> Azad Kashmir is a land of strict curbs on political pluralism, freedom of expression, and freedom of association; a muzzled press; banned books; arbitrary arrest and detention and torture at the hands of the Pakistani military and the police; and discrimination against refugees from Jammu and Kashmir state. Singled out are Kashmiri nationalists who do not support the idea of Kashmir's accession to Pakistan. For those expressing independent or unpopular political views, there is a pervasive fear of Pakistani military and intelligence services—and of militant organizations acting at their behest or independently.

None of this stands true, however, say the locals, if you are a terrorist, an extremist or a member of a banned organisation. This, while Islamabad continues to claim there are curbs on terrorist groups, and that they are banning extremist organisations.

POK, the land of freedom, is becoming every day, a bit more of a free playground for jihadis. On 5 February 2021, the Jaish-e-Mohammed was freely holding a rally in Rawalakot, POK. From the videos, you can see the crowds, the policemen and army people standing amongst the people cheering and shouting slogans. They were shouting that the jihad will go on, challenging the rest of the world to come and see that their struggle would never end. This is not about their struggle for freedom, but for radical Islam. 'The non-Muslims and the agnostic in Pakistan, and specially in Azad Kashmir,' says a local non-believer, 'are seen as people with no right to live. In an organised manner, public service texts are sent to the mobile phones of the general public, in order to tell them that if they know anyone who is ex-Muslim or a non-believer, they should report that person to the police.'

This is also to make sure that the region is kept under the thumb of terrorist organisations ruled by the Army and ISI. In the "Land of Freedom", Kashmiri nationalists who do not support the idea of Kashmir's accession to Pakistan, and people expressing independent or unpopular political views are persecuted, while officially-banned terrorist organisations are allowed to contest elections under different names. Good old Jamaat-ud-Dawa, whose chief is in theory under arrest, has been contesting elections under the name of "United Kashmir Movement", while the anti-Shia terrorist group Sipah-e-Sahaba was contesting under the name of "Rah-e-Haq Party". The banned organisation Tehereek-e-Labbaik Pakistan, the one asking for the beheading and expulsion of the then French Ambassador, was allotted by the Election Commission of Kashmir (PoK) the symbol of "crane" to contest elections.

The lists were available on the internet, until apparently the Ministry of Interior of POK banned Tehereek-e-Labbaik Pakistan's participation under the Terrorism Act. The same Terrorism Act by the way, was generally used to prevent, both in POK and Gilgit Baltistan, the dissenters or those who opposed the ideology, from contesting elections. The Act was also used to jail and torture human rights activists, students and journalists. Needless to say, nobody banned the JuD or Sipah-e-Sahaba. Their goons are everywhere, like JeM goons, and have a capillary control on the territory. 'Whoever wins elections,' says an activist, 'that outcome will not be the expression of the free will of citizens, but of Islamabad's control of the land. They don't need to rig elections, the process is rigged at the root. The only freedom we, citizens of "free" Kashmir have, is the freedom to become members of JuD, JeM or other Islamic extremist organisations. The freedom to go and die for their purposes, to propagate their ideology. For the rest, in the land of freedom, we have no right to speak, no freedom of religion, no freedom of conscience.'

In May 2024, the people living in the "land of freedom" flooded the streets protesting against the government. They protested against the rise in prices and against the injustices daily perpetrated by the Army and the government. Agencies and the Army tried to curb the protests, cutting internet and starting clashes that soon turned deadly. The situation spiralled so much out of control (and the images were anyway released through social media) that in the end, the government was eventually forced to give up.

In November 2024, however, the AJK government promulgated a "Peaceful Assembly and Public Order Ordinance

2024", stating that: "…any gathering or assembly in AJK requires a written application for permission to be submitted to the district magistrate at least seven days in advance." The ordinance resulted in protests and rallies in Rawalakot's Supply Bazaar. 'I belong to Pakistani-occupied Jammu Kashmir, where the pro-Pakistani religious extremist groups are located,' added another activist, 'who recruit teenagers in the name of Islamic jihad, and for the purpose of fighting against Indian forces. They brainwash them, give them limited training, and send them to die in Indian Kashmir. They took benefits from their deaths, for instance, raising funds, and motivating others to do the same. The process continues.'

According to the same local sources and various activists, JeM cadres from Afghanistan have been relocated to Sialkot, Shakargarh, Zaffarwal, Kotli, Bhimber and Muzaffarabad because, 'JeM is currently facing a scarcity of permanent office bearers'. Some of these relocated cadres, according to insiders, have been given the responsibility to look after the "Immamat/Khitabat" of their respective markaz and masjids. While JeM is attempting to regain support and influence within the ISI, the agency itself has been downplaying the role of prominent Pakistan-based organisations like JeM due to international and FATF pressure. Instead, it has sought to give an "indigenous colour" to terror outfits, by promoting Indian local proxies such as Lashkar-e-Mustafa, the Kashmir Tigers (KT), and The Resistance Front (TRF).

The Kashmir Tigers are a quite peculiar group, at least on the surface. Unlike other terror groups such as JeM, Allah Tigers and Hizbul Mujahideen, groups with a strong Islamic ideology, the KT projects a more "secular" and political image. The group was founded by Mufti Altaf (alias Abu Jar), a resident of Anantnag,

South Kashmir, who joined JeM in September 2020. Altaf announced the group's formation in January 2021 via an online video. According to police sources, 'Kashmir Tigers were set up in the post-2019 situation in Kashmir "to show that these had emerged out of local anger with the Indian state" in order "to make their violence more palatable to Western rights activists".'

KT started to make headlines in December 2021, after it claimed responsibility for an attack on a police bus in a highly fortified neighbourhood of Srinagar. In 2024, KT carried out several attacks in J&K against the Army and police, mainly in the once relatively peaceful region of Jammu. It was a tactical and strategic shift for terror groups it appears, in order to keep their assets in the region safe. As a JeM offshoot, the Kashmir Tigers likely relies on JeM's infrastructure, including training camps in Pakistan and Afghanistan. Like TRF, the Kashmir Tigers adopted a non-religious name to project a secular, indigenous image, distancing itself from overtly Islamist groups like JeM, LeT, or Hizbul Mujahideen. This rebranding aligns with Pakistan's strategy to evade scrutiny from the FATF, and portray militancy as a local resistance movement.

According to officials, the revival of old infiltration routes, the diminished deployment of forces in the region, the presence of highly trained terrorists, as well as the decrease of human and technical intelligence networks in the region, are the main reasons why Jammu is seeing a surge in attacks. It proves once more that the good, old, Pakistani strategy is still in place. The activities of terror outfits were in fact, as it always happens, put under the pseudo-control of jihadi outfits by the Islamabad authorities, just for the time necessary to deceive international watchdog organisations. However, as the former RAW Chief Vikram Sood wrote in late April 2025: 'Absence of terrorist attacks should never be mistaken for end of terrorism…. A lull in activity may indicate that militant groups are lying low—regrouping, rebuilding local networks or re-establishing safe houses and arms caches. Conversely, a rise in casualties and clashes does not necessarily suggest that terrorists are gaining the upper hand.'

The moment after Pakistan was removed from the FATF grey list, the pressure on JeM and other terror groups was eased. 'The recent spurt of attacks on Indian security forces and civilians in J&K,' stated a local analyst, 'coupled with the resurgence of terrorist training activities at the Balakot camp, validate the theory that Pakistan's earlier crackdown on these groups was only a strategic deception aimed at misleading the global community.'

POSTSCRIPT
When history writes back

This book began as a report on the Balakot airstrike—and more broadly, is an attempt to trace the decades-long arc of jihadist violence in South Asia, with a particular focus on Jaish-e-Mohammed (JeM). It was meant to be a journalistic account, the sum of years spent reporting, researching, and piecing together the anatomy of militancy in the region. But reality has a habit of rewriting scripts. Just as the manuscript was entering its final review, real-world events intruded into its closing pages.

On 22 April 2025, a gruesome terrorist attack unfolded in Baisaran Valley near Pahalgam, Jammu & Kashmir. Five militants dressed in military fatigues stormed two tourist camps, killing 26 people—25 tourists and a local pony operator. In a devastatingly brutal and premeditated act, the attackers separated the men, demanding they either recite the *Kalima,* the Islamic declarations of faith, or expose themselves. Those unable to comply—particularly uncircumcised individuals—were executed on the spot.

Responsibility was claimed by The Resistance Front (TRF), a known proxy of Lashkar-e-Toiba (LeT) created after the 2019 abrogation of Article 370. The group's leader, Sheikh Sajjad Gul, operating from Pakistan-administered Kashmir, had called for jihad days earlier, alongside LeT commander Abu Musa. Their justification post the attack echoed familiar lines: the victims were labelled "settlers" and "spies"—language that paralleled Pakistani Army Chief General Asim Munir's belligerent speech just a week before, in which he once more referred to Kashmir as Pakistan's "jugular vein".

What followed, however, was also unprecedented. Kashmiris themselves rose—not against New Delhi, but against the terrorists. Shops closed. Strikes were observed. For the first time in living memory, mass protests targeted jihadists rather than the State. A line had been crossed. War-weary and economically invested in tourism and pilgrimage, the people of Kashmir made it clear that they would not be used as cannon fodder ever again.

Indian intelligence estimates that roughly 100 well-trained militants remain active in the region. Notably, the Pahalgam attackers carried not just AK-47s, but US-made M4 carbines—weapons not commonly seen in South Asian insurgencies. These likely originated from the $7 billion worth of American arms left behind in Afghanistan after the 2021 US withdrawal. Many have since surfaced in Pakistan, in the hands of ISI-backed groups.

On 7 May, India launched "Operation Sindoor" a calibrated response involving surgical strikes on nine terror facilities across Pakistan and Pakistan-administered Kashmir. Among the most significant targets were Muridke, the Lashkar-e-Toiba headquarters, and Bahawalpur, JeM's base of operations.

The most consequential outcome was the confirmed death of Abdul Rauf Asghar, JeM's de facto leader and the brother of Masood Azhar. Also killed were ten other members of the Azhar family. Jaish itself acknowledged the loss, with Masood Azhar confirming the deaths at Subhan Allah Markaz in Bahawalpur.

In Muridke, multiple senior LeT operatives were killed, including Mudassar Khadian Khas (aka Abu Jundal), head of Markaz Taiba. The funerals for these figures were not held in secret—quite the opposite. Pakistani Army personnel, civil officials, police, and members of the banned Jamaat-ud-Dawa (JuD), openly attended. Mudassar received a full guard of honour, with wreaths reportedly laid on behalf of the Pakistan Army Chief and Punjab's Chief Minister.

Despite Pakistan's predictable denials—insisting once again, that "there are no terrorist camps in Pakistan"—and its disinformation campaign accusing India of targeting civilians, the facts this time spoke far louder than spun narratives. Unlike the ambiguity that clouded the Balakot strike in 2019, this time, the evidence was overwhelming. Masood Azhar's own admission of family casualties, visual confirmation of the targeted sites, and most strikingly, the public, State-sanctioned funerals attended by army personnel, intelligence officials, and provincial authorities, left no room for plausible deniability.

In the end, this book was overtaken by the speed and weight of unfolding events. And it has become, unavoidably, a work of recent history. A history that refuses to stay buried in files and footnotes, because the story it tells is still being lived—in blood, rhetoric, and the shifting balance of power across borders that remain hot, disputed, and haunted.